OATMEAL ON MY BLAZER:

HAVING IT ALL AND OTHER MYTHS

By: Rochelle Lamm Wallach with Linda M. Koe

Published by Panache Publications, Appleton, Wisconsin.

Cover art and illustrations by award winning artist, Ellen Anderson. Ellen
owns and operates her own successful illustration and card company in
Milwaukee, Wisconsin. Her fanciful illustrations reflect her personal
experiences as a working mother of three youngsters.

ISBN: 0-9633304-0-3

Printed in the United States of America   August, 1992

Oatmeal On My Blazer:
Having It All And Other Myths

Table Of Contents

DEDICATION

Oatmeal On My Blazer is dedicated with great affection to my mother, Marion Lamm.

My mother was a pioneer working woman, long before debates of whether you could have it all or not were in vogue. I'm not sure she really knows how far ahead of her time she really was.

She was a pioneer of adventurous honeymoons decades before they became fashionable. No cruise to Bermuda or grand tour of Europe for her. She and my father headed north to the Canadian bush in his little two-seater Piper Cub days after their wedding. They honeymooned at a deserted mink trapper's shack, where they began chopping down trees and clearing bush to build the multi-million dollar luxury resort business that would dominate their married life together.

She was a pioneer in entrepreneurial endeavors, ages before the National Association of Women Business Owners or Women In Management organizations came into existence. Working side-by-side with my dad, she helped create one of the best known hunting and fishing lodges and bush airline operations in all of Canada. With no college education to guide her, she let sheer energy, determination, and "women's intuition" pilot her in this endeavor.

She was a pioneer working mother who raised her brood of five daughters seventy miles from the nearest doctor, armed only with a dog-eared edition of Dr. Spock. When she was almost six months pregnant with me, she was featured on the cover of *Sports Afield* magazine holding aloft a twenty-five pound Muskie. The photo was taken at dusk after a full day of baking and cooking over a wood burning stove for the Norwegian lumberjack crew and Ojibwa Indians helping with lodge construction. The byline (written by an editor unaware of her "condition") extolled the benefits of the healthy and carefree north country.

She was a pioneer in customer service and the red-carpet treatment for guests, well before it became the buzz word for every marketer in America. She had her eye on every detail of lodge operations long before the Malcolm Baldrige Quality Service Award was created and certainly before Walt Disney conceived or executed the pristine grounds of Disneyland. Every evening every ketchup bottle in the place was washed and the tops run through the dishwasher to ensure a "new" bottle for each new diner. Mom personally checked and garnished every plate that went into the dining room for thirty summers to ensure that each plate was perfect. (To this day, I cringe when a plate is served in a restaurant with a drip.) Her devotion to detail and her commitment to excellence would be the envy of any Fortune 500 CEO.

My mother has been a pioneer all her life. And all the time, I don't think that she has ever recognized just how extraordinary her accomplishments have been. But the five Lamm daughters, and especially me, have always known we could accomplish anything - because she did.

INTRODUCTION

The overview.

●In 1986 I turned forty.

●In 1986 I was named president of the mutual fund subsidiary of one of the largest life insurance companies in the United States.

●In 1986 I paid more in federal income taxes than the highest annual salary that, even in my wildest imagination, I had ever hoped to make.

Now there's nothing unusual about turning forty. Thousands of women do that every day.

And there's nothing truly unusual about being named the President of a company. The press reports these announcements regularly.

And there's nothing very unusual either about paying a lot of taxes. I'm in very good company there. In the twenty years that I've been working, Congress has seen fit to change the tax code more often than Cher changes her hairstyle, and each time most of us have been on the receiving end of a higher tax bill.

What is unusual, however, is that any of these things, or any of the successes that I have been fortunate to enjoy, could have been achieved by Rochelle Lamm Wallach, a young woman (I've found that your perception of what constitutes young changes when you cross the threshold of forty) who grew up in what most people would probably describe as a small hick pulp and paper mill town of 10,000 and graduated from an all-girls' high school class of sixty-two. Since I

3

began my career after high school as a Roman Catholic nun, I don't think that I'm the only one who is surprised by this turn of events. I'm not sure that anyone in my home town ever expected anything very much of me career-wise.

This then is the story of how I - a forty-three year-old investment industry executive, running a company that will post over one quarter of a billion dollars in sales this year, through one of the largest national mutual fund sales forces (2,300 Registered Representatives) in the country - have tried to keep all the balls in the air: executive, wife, mother.

With the prestige and financial rewards that have come with my career through the years, I sense that lots of people probably think that I'm as close to having it all as anyone could be. I live in a wonderful, big sprawling home with a panoramic view of the Fox River, drive a new Cadillac every few years, indulged myself by buying a full length mink coat the winter I received my promotion to the executive VP ranks, and keep my house running with the help of a terrific college-educated nanny, plus a gardener and full time housekeeper; am married to a handsome attorney who thinks I'm the best thing since the invention of the television remote control, and am mother to a wonderful red-headed little seven-year-old boy named David-Andrew. I also have all the worries, guilt, pressures, conflicts, and terminal fatigue that go hand-in-hand with trying to have it all.

The following pages are dedicated to women everywhere who work outside the home because you know what I'm talking about. *Oatmeal On My Blazer* is for everyone of you. You are the unsung heroines who slug it out in the trenches daily. You type letters, sell real estate, answer phones, manage staffs of people, raise kids, operate machinery, drive trucks, run corporations, clean bathrooms, cook meals, send birthday cards to your in-laws, make martinis for your husbands, prepare annual budgets, and pay the electric bills - and not necessarily in that order. For all you do, this book's for you!

4

CHAPTER 1. WHAT GLASS CEILING?

Putting some cracks in the theory.

I sense history will record that some of the most heated debates of the twentieth century centered around issues of women in business, women in politics, women in any position of authority and/or power. Notwithstanding the thousands of bras which seem to have been burned in vain since the days of the Suffragettes, chauvinism still seems to be alive and well in many circles where there continues to exist a prevailing notion that a woman absolutely cannot be President of the United States of America because she might have PMS and push the hot button and bomb Cuba or something.

Personally, I'll take my chances anytime with a capable woman high on Midol over some of the clowns who have graced our capitol and our front pages in the last few Washington administrations. I'm not a booster of Geraldine Ferraro, who made an interesting run for the vice-presidency in 1984, but even on her worst day she came off like a rocket scientist when lined up against the likes of Spiro Agnew!

This chauvinistic line of reasoning would continue then to suggest that a woman cannot possibly head a multi-million dollar, Fortune-500-type company because her judgment might be clouded by all that estrogen racing through her system - like the guys running Exxon are paragons of good judgement (just witness the handling of the Valdez incident).

Coming from an unconventional line of strong females (my grandmother went on the road as a traveling coffee "salesman" sixty-seven years ago in 1925 - long before the first Suffragette burned her bra - and for thirty years my mother, while raising a brood of five daughters, put in sixteen- and eighteen-hour days as a partner with my father, to build one of the largest and best known hunting and fishing lodges and bush airline operations in northwestern Ontario, Canada), it just never even occurred to me that women were intellectually or in any other sense inferior to men.

Over the course of my twenty years in business, I've been committed to forging myself to the top financially and professionally. During this time I've run up against some real died-in-the-wool chauvinists and happily have had the good fortune to prove them wrong about their lousy theories often enough times to even the score.

My determination to land a corner office and CEO credentials probably had its genesis, in part at least, during my childhood in Kenora, Ontario, Canada. Growing up in that small paper-mill town, definitely located off the beaten path in the middle of Canada, I spent six months each year at our family's hunting and fishing resort seventy miles from the closest town. The extent of my cultural exposure was spending Saturday nights dancing with our Indian fishing guides and bush pilots, most of whom were in the sauce most of the time. These humble beginnings taught me some invaluable lessons, such as how to cook the best darn Walleye shore lunch in the North Woods, but it also motivated me to carve out a more cosmopolitan existence for myself as an adult.

Choosing never to see the glass ceiling others bemoan, I have chosen rather to see only the sky as my limit. Through a combination of plain old hard work and lots of lucky breaks along the way, I've been able to stack up a few accomplishments that for many women might seem absolutely unattainable (and which, frankly, have surprised the heck out of me from time to time). My six years as an executive vice-president for one of the, then, most prominent New York Stock Exchange member firms in the country easily earned for me over a million dollars.

In 1986, the year I turned forty, I was named president of the mutual fund subsidiary of one of the largest life insurance companies in the country. My career has presented me with some fabulous opportunities (four years of commuting to New York City exposed me to life in the fast lane, the best hotels, most expensive restaurants, finest French wines, and stretchiest limos) as well as lots of interesting challenges - opportunities and challenges that I never dreamed of growing up in the Canadian bush.

Then, something happened seven years ago that forever changed, and continues to challenge, me. A month before my thirty-eighth birthday I had my first baby - a boy, David-Andrew. Believe me, John Sculley and Lee Iaccoca have never been tested as I have been tested. These prominent gentlemen run huge corporate complexes while the "little woman" runs the home front - just as God intended it to be. In contrast, I run a multi-million dollar brokerage and mutual fund organization by day as super-executive, and then I shift gears each evening to become super-mom and super-wife when I leave the office. This gear shifting process is not always accomplished smoothly.

I mean, really, would Donald Trump nurse (even assuming he had the right equipment) his four week-old son at the office while at the same time paring an extra hundred thousand or so out of an unbalanced year end operating budget and conducting a cross-country conference call with six area vice-presidents looking for direction from the top about how to sell the company's common stock fund when the equity market has just plummeted thirty percent in the past thirty-six hours? Talk about the art of the deal!!

I'm a woman who is easily bored (I never know what to do when I go to a symphony concert) so I really do relish my multiple family and professional roles. However, there have been times when my wires have gotten crossed, the roles have overlapped, and the results have probably raised an eyebrow or two.

Take last Thursday for example. I was rushing through Chicago's O'Hare airport to catch the last flight home. I hadn't checked with the office since noon and needed to pick up my messages from our automated voice mail system just to make sure that my first two early morning breakfast meetings the next day were still on. (Yes, on some days, to get it all done, back-to-back morning meals get scheduled. After awhile that all-American breakfast - juice, toast, hash browns, bacon and eggs - starts to look about as appealing as the eel and seaweed sushi someone tried to foist on me once. Black coffee is often all that I can manage to choke down.)

After plopping down my hanging garment bag, briefcase and latest issue of *Forbes*, I dug into my purse for my AT&T credit card to make the call while cradling the phone on my shoulder. Until the break up of Ma Bell, I used to be clever enough to make long distance calls. Now I'm not so sure.

As a matter of fact, in my view, the telecommunication technological "revolution" seems to be getting entirely out of hand. Not only do Sprint, MCI, and AT&T do their darnedest to confuse you about rates, services and equipment (life is no longer as easy as waiting in line for twenty minutes for a phone to free up - now you have to make sure you're in the right line for the right phone company's equipment!), but our corporate telecommunications department insists on changing our phone calling card numbers every year for "security" reasons or some such nonsense. This means that for the first nine months of every year I need the card in front of me each time I make a call, but don't tell them.

I think they change these numbers every twelve months as some sort of corporate IQ test. The logic seems to be that if you can memorize a new calling card number each year (completely erasing from your memory banks the old one), as well as remember the six digit access number to AT&T, the phone number to your office, your computerized voice mailbox number, plus your personal security code number - well, if you can do all that, then you're probably smart enough to run the company!

In any case, I punched the thirty-two digits into the phone and, as my messages began to replay, I scrounged at the bottom of my purse for something to write with. What did I come up with? Not a Mont Blanc fountain pen, not even the engraved Cross pen that the Business and Professional Women's chapter had given me when I gave the keynote address at their regional conference. No way. What I was clutching was a red Crayola crayon, and one with a slightly chewed tip at that. Every mother on earth knows that keeping sufficient art materials at hand to entertain the junior members of the household is a prerequisite for mummyhood, at least until the youngest child reaches the age of about nineteen at which time they should be able to carry their own provisions for marking on restaurant napkins.

As smartly dressed young executives and salesmen in their crisp white Brooks Brothers' button-down shirts and razor haircuts lined up on either side of me at the bank of phones, there I was, president of the third largest mutual fund organization in Wisconsin, taking notes on the back of an envelope with one of my son's red crayons. Binney & Smith would have been so proud. Harold Geneen, on the other hand, would probably have cringed.

CHAPTER 2. MY BIOLOGICAL CLOCK WAS TICKING

Or was that a bomb?

"Rochelle, pick up line one; it's a Dr. Higgins' office calling. Says it's personal."

Teresa, my secretary of five years, was great at screening my calls. But this call was one I'd asked her to put right through.

Kerry Higgins, my general family practice physician, was calling. Dr. Higgins was the one I consulted on all matters medical in nature from a stiff neck to that mortifying case of scabies that I picked up the one and only time I chanced to use the ladies' hot tub at the health club I joined.

I crossed my fingers. This was the call I had been waiting for, the phone call that would confirm whether my suspicions were correct that the weekend spent with Alan in Hawaii had produced more than two cases of sunburn.

"Are you sitting down? Your lab work just came back. You're pregnant."

Oh, my gosh. Holy smokes. A rabbit had just died in my honor!

"Thank you, Kerry, thanks a lot. I'll get an appointment set up right away with an OB. Oh, wait . . . just a minute, don't hang up. Any idea how far along I am?"

"Well, you never can be positive about these things, Rochelle, and your obstetrician will have a better idea after he sees you the first time, but it looks like you'll be having a Valentine's Day baby."

Placing the telephone receiver slowly in its cradle, I got up from my desk and closed my office door. Whew, I needed to let this all sink in. What a phone call. Ma Bell really did her best today. Talk about reach out and touch someone.

A Valentine's Day baby. How amazing . . . and sweet. A little cherub of my own . . . our own . . . to be born on Valentine's Day.

This was all the more special to me since my marriage to Alan was probably not the most conventional. Face it, former Catholic nuns who have become traveling business executives that commute biweekly from Denver to New York for their jobs and are married to divorced Jewish attorneys with two grown children from a prior marriage are not exactly a dime a dozen. Certainly my expectation of this exceptional union was for a child who was absolutely out of the ordinary as well.

Well, having a Valentine baby was certainly special. Valentine's Day evoked thoughts of hearts and flowers and sweets and love and romance. The connection that I did not immediately make is that February 14 is also the anniversary of the Valentine's Day massacre! This would occur to me later . . . much later.

I was pregnant! Egads! Now what? While flooded with emotion, handling this with cool-headed, sophisticated aplomb was critical, I told myself. I can't let the fact that I am in the process of creating another human being change the clear headed, unemotional way that I conduct business. It just wouldn't be professional, and professional demeanor has always been important to me.

OK, fine, there were the years when as Sister Mary Michol I was devoting my life to the Congregation of the Sisters of Good Shepherd as a nun. But even then, I wanted nothing more than to be a really top-notch professional nun - not a bubble-headed-Sally-Fields-type flying nun - that would have been much too frivolous an image for me. My idea of the "right" kind of nun was the level-headed, rather stern Mother Superior in The Sound of Music. Now there was a professional woman!

After my stint in the convent in St. Paul, Minnesota in the late sixties, I had a few years of readjustment to secular life as a college coed. This resembled a slightly looser form of convent life since I had chosen to attend an all-girls', Catholic college. Upon graduation I made a rather significant career change and entered the world of business. You might say that my transition was, in a literal sense, from broadcloth to boardroom. Deciding that for me it was infinitely more challenging (and absolutely more financially worthwhile) to make my way in the secular world than the cloister, I chose what many would agree might just be the most challenging arena of all, the world of high finance, mega deals and billion dollar transactions: Wall Street. In other words, the wild and oft times wacky world of the investment industry.

It occurred to me, as I took the first job I'd ever had where I didn't wear a habit, that it might be difficult for a fresh faced former nun to be taken seriously. So I read *Things Mother Never Told You* and *Working Woman* and *Savvy* magazines, everything that was supposed to help a working girl get ahead. And they all said in one way or another, acting like a professional would almost certainly stand you in good stead.

So with "professional demeanor" as one of the credos of my business life, I started out in the secretarial pool. By the time I took that important call from Dr. Higgins' office in 1984, I'd worked my way up the corporate ladder to executive vice-president and national sales manager of one of the subsidiaries of a prominent New York Stock Exchange member company. The whole time I held firm to my carefully developed hard-driving executive "persona."

This was serious stuff, investing other people's money. Well, it wasn't money really, it was more than that. It was people's hopes and dreams. Little old ladies in Omaha trusted us with their life savings. Young couples just starting out trusted us with the first few thousand dollars they had, with the hope that we could help them send their toddlers to a top-notch college someday. It was imperative that their money be entrusted to professionals. Therefore it was imperative that I steadfastly maintain the professional demeanor that warranted their trust.

I would tell the young women CPAs and attorneys joining our firm who sought my counsel (and flattered me with their suggestions that I was their role model for career success), "If you really want to make it to the executive suite, first: act like a lady and work like a dog; second: live, breathe, sleep, and eat like a professional. Never let your guard down. You can't afford to. This is a male dominated industry. To be taken seriously you've got to have a polished and professional image."

So there I was, an MBA, one of three distinguished alumni from the University of Denver Graduate School of Business, an executive vice-president of a respected Wall Street firm, a successful financial marketing maven with a hard earned reputation as a hard-driving business executive - clearly a professional. I didn't know then as I finished the phone call with Dr. Higgins that the true test of my professionalism was just about to begin.

I was thrilled. I was elated. I was overjoyed. I was going to have it all - a fabulous career, a handsome and devoted husband, and now a precious baby. Everyone knows that most first impressions are just that. FIRST impressions. Boy, was I in for a rude awakening!

Sinking back into my swivel chair I didn't know what to do first. Now, I've never been able to keep a secret longer than twenty seconds, and this was no time to change styles. I had to tell someone. NOW. So right away I called Alan. He was thrilled . . . and proud. Nothing so strokes the male ego as knowing that his sperm are still potent.

"Now, Rochelle, don't expect me to change diapers. I'm too old to change diapers."

Great, already he was setting down the ground rules for his version of fatherhood. I raise the kid until Alan can start taking him to baseball games and then "Mr. Mom" will step in and show me what real parenting is.

Then I called my mother. She was stunned.

"You're kidding. Oh, my God. I can't deal with this right now. I'll have to call you back."

Oh, good. Instant guilt and the fetus is barely as big as the birth control pill I was no longer taking.

Well, I guess Mom had a right to be shocked. After all, this unusual announcement was coming from her liberated, executive-career daughter who had never once hinted that she had any interest in activities that were even remotely domestic. This announcement was coming from the only one of her five daughters who had subscribed to W. C. Field's philosophy, "Anyone who hates kids and dogs can't be all bad."

This was the daughter who had never once played with dolls. Instead, at age five, I'd started my first business "empire." At the end of each day I would visit our Indian fishing guides and scoop up all the dead minnows they were going to throw away. Then I'd go cabin-to-cabin selling my day-old salted dead bait to our lodge guests, undercutting my dad's live bait price by seventy-five cents a dozen. It was a sweet deal while it lasted - about a week - before my dad got wind of my little venture.

I was still excited. I still needed to let someone else hear my great news. I started to call my boss. Hmmm. Paralysis set in. I could not lift the phone. What would he say? What would he think? He'd be worried about how this would affect my performance, my ability to continue to run my operation effectively. He'd be afraid that I'd be distracted by my new role and responsibilities as a mother and give less time and attention to the company. He wouldn't like this at all. He'd put me on the Mommy Track.

And how would my staff and the rest of the company react? Would being pregnant change their perception of me as a hard driving executive? Would they see me now as just another woman with a "bun in the oven?" Well, I'd never been pregnant before, so how did I know how anyone would react?

So I made my first pregnant executive decision. I decided I just wouldn't tell anyone at the office for a while. I'd continue to work my fanny off to reinforce just what an indispensable executive I was. When I finally tell the boss, I decided, I'd outline exactly how I would manage "my new executive baby" and how this would not interfere one little bit with my ability to commute every other week between my New York and Denver offices to keep the company humming along. No problem.

And for the first twelve weeks of my pregnancy, it wasn't - too much.

Happily, I was blessed with a cast iron stomach that eliminated the nausea and morning sickness that can plague some women so I continued my normal hectic schedule including 7:15 a.m. breakfast appointments most mornings without the need to camp out in the loo afterwards. So, except for the fact that I was putting on a little weight (more about that later), from all outward appearances I was the same business person I had always been.

I also didn't want to encounter the inevitable office gossip that goes along with the announcement of a pregnancy. It seemed best to delay telling folks until I absolutely had to.

"So when are you going to tell them?" Alan kept asking.

"Soon."

"You've been saying that for three months now. You really need to tell the office. They need to know so they can plan around the time that you'll be out."

"Out! What do you mean out? Alan, I'm just taking ten days, or at the most two weeks, to have this baby. We'll hire the nanny; I'll have the baby. Place the baby in the nanny's capable arms and head back to the office. Really this is not going to be a big deal. I think this whole pregnancy and childbirth thing gets blown all out of proportion sometimes. I don't want to do that."

Well, really, what was the big deal? Legend has it that American pioneer women would just squat at the side of the farm field, have the baby, and thirty minutes later commence plowing again. If they could do it, so could I. Today's women had gone soft. I would be the pioneer female executive that would show them, and corporate America in general, how this baby thing was done.

"You may be right. But I still think that you ought to say something to your boss."

So, two months later, when I was five-months pregnant, and about to pop out of my clothes, I decided that Alan was right and made my announcement.

CHAPTER 3. YOU'RE WHAT?

Dropping the bomb.

"We're still on for three o'clock. See you in Arthur's office."

This sound bite was coming from Jay Chazanoff, the senior executive vice president to whom I reported, as he quickly poked his head in and then out of my office to confirm our meeting later in the day. After this enlightening bit of news, Jay continued down the hall on his rounds.

I'd flown into New York earlier that morning from Denver for my monthly sixty-minute meeting with Arthur Goldberg, CEO of our parent firm, and Jay,

Arthur's right hand man with whom I had been working for the better part of a year in connection with the start up of our stock and bond money management activities.

After Jay had left, I reflected on last month's meeting with the two "head Freds." It had certainly been eventful. Right in the middle of my animated presentation of what I had in mind for our new advertising campaign, one of the uniformed security guards hurriedly rushed in, cutting me off mid-sentence, to announce that the building was being evacuated and we would have to leave pronto. It seems that more than 100 of New York's finest police and fire fighters were congregating in the lobby because of a bomb threat - a not infrequent event in New York City.

As Jay and Arthur and I joined the other denizens of our building and trudged down the stairwell twenty-two flights to Forty-second Street, Arthur remarked, "Just once, I'd like to give a piece of my mind to the jerks who make these bomb threats. This is a blasted inconvenience."

"Not as inconvenient as being dead would be, Arthur," I shot back.

"That would really foul up our business plan. Anyway, did you ever think that maybe this is just one of our limited partner's way of conveying that they're a little unhappy about the way their highly leveraged equipment leasing investment worked out?"

Well, today's meeting was going to involve a type of bomb too. I was ready to drop a real bombshell.

I had mentally rehearsed my pregnancy announcement presentation (I thought of it this way, as though it were one of my stand-up, knock-em-dead, investment seminars) for days. It needed to convey to Arthur and Jay the fact that this pregnancy would be no more inconvenient than having a hang nail, and that certainly it would not affect in the least my ability to launch our new mutual fund family successfully and right on schedule. I wanted to make sure that Arthur understood how committed I was to running my business without interruption, just as I always had.

Having this baby, I would assure them, would affect the company no more than my taking a two-week vacation (which, of course, I had never done in my five years of affiliation with them because who would take care of things if I were away for that long? Talk about delusions of grandeur.) I can't believe I was so naive about all this, but, there you have it, I was!

In between phone calls, two interviews for a new customer service manager, a quick trip to Madison Avenue to look over the graphic designs for our new marketing brochure and a heated battle with our law firm about their tardiness in completing the contracts with one of our data processing suppliers, I kept mentally rehearsing what I would say. During lunch - well, if you can call washing down two-thirds of a tuna salad sandwich with a half-pint of warm skim milk at my desk lunch - I jotted down my main points on a yellow legal pad just to impress myself that I was really prepared for this meeting.

So, what's the worst that could happen, I asked myself.

The way I figured it, this news was either going to go over like a lead balloon, in which case I'd be hoofing it up and down Wall Street trying to peddle myself as a highly capable, albeit slightly pregnant, sales manager desperately in need of work; or Jay and Arthur would both go into shock in which case I'd only need a few minutes to administer smelling salts to revive them, and life would go on as usual. I doubted that once I'd sprung my news, they would want to prolong our meeting trading tidbits about booties and formula options. The odds were that this would be a short meeting.

From what I can tell, every working woman who becomes pregnant faces with more than a modest degree of trepidation the nerve-wracking dilemma of "'fessing up" to her boss. This is a uniquely female experience. There is absolutely no equivalent male counter-experience to compare with this need to convey to your superior, who is undoubtedly male, that you are busy creating a new life for the planet, and therefore the company will need to limp along without your services for the six weeks of your maternity leave while you try to cope with new motherhood before returning to the hallowed halls of corporate enterprise.

Pregnancy announcements have been known to be met with stony stares or even disapproving frowns, or - sometimes even worse - condescending good humor. Starting or adding to your family is generally seen as a sign that you aren't really that serious about your career or dedicated to the company or you would have kept a tighter rein on your reproductive urges. No good-old-boy "atta boy" slap on the back when you break this news.

Hordes of working women have come back from maternity leaves to find that their jobs no longer exist at all, having been eliminated in a corporate down sizing, or that some far junior "golden boy" has catapulted himself four rungs up the corporate ladder in their absence and is now well ensconced in what used to be their slot in the organization chart. No wonder it produces such anxieties to anticipate "The Announcement."

However, Mother Nature is totally unconcerned with any of these bureaucratic ramifications. She keeps on increasing our girth, both below and above the waist (an ever expanding bosom is one of the real benefits of pregnancy I learned), to the point that some admission of pregnancy must ultimately be made.

That is unless the woman happens to be one of those folks that make tabloid headlines such as WOMAN DELIVERS BABY AT STOCK CAR RACES: "WE DIDN'T KNOW SHE WAS PREGNANT," PIT CREW REACTS. These women were either grossly overweight to start with and under the impression that menopause sets in during your thirties - hence no periods for nine months - or masters of disguise. Being none of these, I nervously prepared for my moment of truth which was fast approaching as the hands on my desk clock moved closer to 3:00 p.m.

At 2:57 p.m. I mentally rehearsed my key points one last time:

1. Plans for the new product launch are right on track.
2. We are on time with all phases.
   -Prospectus filed with Securities and Exchange Commission.
   -Transfer agency and custodian agreements in place.
   -Computer programming well under way.
   -Marketing plans and sales literature are designed and ready to go on press.
   -Advertising and public relations agencies hired.
3. The March 1 deadline looks good.
4. We have a few personnel issues to iron out.
5. I love my job.
6. My commitment to the firm is stronger than ever.
7. I'm pregnant.
8. I feel great.
9. My doctor appointments are all in the evenings. They won't interfere with business at all.
10. I'm due February 14.
11. I'm hiring a nanny.
12. I'll be back in the office no later than February 24.
13. This is no big deal.
14. Having this baby will not affect my performance in the least. I am totally committed to running my business without interruption.

Item number fourteen was the one I really wanted to stress since I felt it was absolutely critical to leave a very strong impression with Jay and Arthur that I realized how important I was to the firm and that they didn't have to worry in the least that I would leave them or the company in the lurch. As it turned out, that should have been the least of my concerns - but that's a later chapter.

I waited until the clock was at 3:03 p.m. before I headed for Arthur's office. Walking down the spiral staircase to the executive suite on the floor below, my knees got stronger; my heart rate increased slightly, and I started to get that adrenaline flow that always precedes my striding confidently onto the platform to conduct an investment sales training workshop.

Passing by Madeleine, Arthur's secretary, I poked my head through his open door. Jay had arrived. Arthur was finishing a phone call and waved me onto the sofa by the window. "Be done in a minute," he mouthed wordlessly. I started to pour myself a cup of coffee from Arthur's built-in executive wet bar, remembered that caffeine was a no-no for pregnant moms, decided against it and plopped down on the leather sofa by Jay.

I'd been in this office dozens of times. We'd hashed over strategy, debated new product features, made heart-wrenching personnel decisions, argued, agreed, been angry with one another, and laughed together about deals that worked out just the way we had expected they would. I'd never had such a knot in the pit of my stomach as I had right now. I'd rather impart the intimate details of my sex life, I thought, or tell them about all the skeletons in my closet, or admit I might have splurged on my expense account once when I ordered a bottle of wine through room service to celebrate a big sale. I'd rather tell them ANYTHING right now rather than, "I'm pregnant."

Arthur hung up and came over to join us, sitting down in the matching leather club chair. He and Jay both turned my way, obviously expecting me to kick off the discussion.

"Arthur, Jay, here's the rundown on where we are with the new funds."

I pulled out my yellow pad. I've never used a written outline, or even a note of any kind, even when speaking in front of an audience of hundreds of investors, but somehow it seemed comforting to have this yellow pad in front of me for this presentation.

As I expounded on item number one on my agenda, Arthur's secretary, Madeleine, buzzed him with a phone call. He told her to take a message and looked back at me to continue. Moving on to item number two, Geoff Bobroff, our firm's new administrative guru, poked his head into the office to see when Arthur would be available to talk about the new accounting system they were installing.

Following a brief exchange, Geoff closed the door again and Arthur and Jay attentively faced me once more. I moved onto the next item, matter of factly describing our progress with the new funds, all the while feeling as though I was going to gag at any moment. I had almost finished item number three before Madeleine walked into the office with a pile of correspondence for Arthur to sign while we talked.

With each interruption I became more anxious. It was getting harder and harder to concentrate. This meeting was taking forever!! At this rate I was never going to get the news out. Finally I was on item number four.

"We've got a couple of interesting personnel matters to iron out before we can launch this new fund. I'm not sure whether Jack is really right for the Eastern region, and we definitely need to hire another assistant for the portfolio service director. She is absolutely swamped."

As Arthur and Jay discussed Jack's merits and whether the portfolio service director was really overworked or just whiny, I was mentally having an anxiety attack. I couldn't stand it anymore.

"Look, Jay, there's another personnel matter to consider. I've got a little staffing situation I need to fill you in on. We're going to be expanding rather unexpectedly."

Arthur and Jay were both staring at me with mild interest.

Taking a deep breath, I told myself, "This is it, just TELL them."

"I'm going to have a baby."

Arthur and Jay continued to stare at me. Arthur looked dumbfounded. Jay's jaw fell open. They were in no position to respond, so I babbled on filling the conversational void.

"Jay, Arthur, having a baby won't affect anything here in New York. I love my job, I'm hiring a nanny, and I'm not going to miss a beat in getting the new funds launched. This is really no big deal, and I don't want to blow it out of proportion. In fact I wouldn't have even said anything except I just thought I should say something so that you wouldn't be curious when I start to wear maternity clothes in the next day or two. I'm totally committed to the firm, and this is not going to interrupt my running my business in the slightest."

Jay finally stammered and stuttered, "Well, that IS an interesting personnel matter."

Jay unfolded his legs and picked up his Day-Timer. Arthur rose from the leather chair and headed back to his desk. I was right. The meeting was over and it had been short.

Arthur stopped, turned around and said, "So what are you going to do?"

"Well, I'm going to take two weeks off and have a baby, hire a nanny, and be back at work before you've even noticed that I'm gone," I cavalierly replied.

Nodding in seeming agreement with my sentiments, Arthur continued to his desk.

"Thanks for telling us. Keep us posted."

This had not gone exactly as I had planned - not unlike most of the events that would be associated with my pregnancy - but at least it was over. Telling myself that I would have other occasions before February 14 to speak more eloquently with Arthur and Jay to convince them that my being pregnant was not going to be a corporate liability, I rose and walked toward the door. I had come out of the closet, so to speak. I could now tell my staff. More importantly, I could shop for maternity clothes and finally get into something comfortable.

For the past three weeks I'd ruined every leather belt I owned. When my waist expanded and I finally got to the last notch, I had to punch new holes to loosen my belt a half-inch at a time. The problem was, I was adding a new notch about every 18 hours.

As I exited Arthur's office, he looked up from his desk and said, "Oh, by the way, Rochelle, when's the baby due?"

I was in the hall by now. I turned back to face Arthur and replied, "February 14, Arthur, I'm having a Valentine's Day baby."

Madeleine, sitting at her secretarial station outside Arthur's door, and ever alert for any tantalizing office scuttlebutt fit to spread (and some that wasn't) looked at me.

"Baby? Who's having a baby?"

"Me, Madeleine, in February."

Disbelief crossed her face. Here I was, almost thirty-eight years-old, purported role model for scores of women coming up through the ranks anxious to crash through the glass ceiling, one hundred percent committed to my career and having conveyed zero interest in anything remotely connected to family matters. I had confessed all of these things freely to all who knew me. No wonder she was surprised. She wasn't the only one.

As I walked back into my office, Annette, the secretary I shared with our portfolio manager during the weeks I worked in my New York office, was just putting down the phone. "Rochelle, you've got some telephone messages on your desk."

"Thanks, Annette."

I returned Pam LaMarsh's call first.

"Rochelle, I just heard! I knew you were pregnant. I've been watching your ankles expand for the last ninety days and I just knew it. It had to be. Madeleine says you're due on Valentine's Day."

If only Gannet could get a patent on Madeleine. She was better than a bill board.

"Aren't you excited? Or are you? Like, was this planned?"

Good grief. Was this planned? Was the Hindenberg planned? No this was not planned. But it was certainly not unwelcome. Not unwelcome at all. I was sincerely thrilled at the prospect of motherhood and equally determined that it was not going to affect my precious career in the least.

Back in my Denver office the next morning, I asked my secretary to come in.

"Teresa, round up the staff and get them all together at 10:00 a.m."

I wanted to tell them my news before someone else let the cat out of the bag. This was my staff of three years who had worked like crazy to help me build our asset management company from scratch into one of the premier organizations in the country. They'd developed into a close knit team and I knew it was important for me to personally break the news and assure them that this latest development wouldn't interfere with our operations in the least.

"It's going to be business as usual," I announced.

What an innocent I was.

Reactions to the announcement were interesting to say the least. My staff was wonderful. Never once did they intimate that I was naive in the extreme to think that my advancing pregnancy or coping with a new baby would in any way change the way I had done business for years. They continued to do their jobs as usual and simply waited for the other shoe to fall.

During my next New York stint, one of my male colleagues with whom I had traded friendly barbs at the coffee machine for years poked his head into my office.

"Boy, am I glad you're pregnant. I thought you were just getting FAT."

"And I thought all along that you asked your barber to cut your hair so that you looked like a fourteenth century monk. That little bald place is SO interesting. Thanks so much for stopping in, Creighton. You have really made my day."

Creighton chuckled as he left the office.

In the past I'd been told by Teresa that many of the secretaries and clerks in the firm (who were of course overwhelmingly female) found me intimidating. This always surprised me because I think of myself as very approachable. (Just goes to show you how little we know about ourselves sometimes.) As much as I hate to admit it, there must have been some truth to her observations, however, because I had noticed that whenever I would walk into our word processing department or pass by a gaggle of file clerks, suddenly all conversation would cease and a hush would fall over the group.

Once my pregnancy became common knowledge - which took less than 36 hours (it would have been quicker than that but some folks were out of the office on business or vacation when I made the announcement and it took a few extra hours for the grapevine to catch up with them) - all barriers of "rank" disappeared and I was no longer viewed as an executive. I became "just one of the girls."

My pregnancy became a great equalizer. Secretaries, who had hardly as much as acknowledged my "good morning" in the past, would tell me how keeping soda crackers at their desks to munch on helped stave off morning sickness (usually), and how they hated using the elevators during the final months of pregnancy because they felt claustrophobic, or who their obstetrician was and how well (or awfully) he/she handled their last delivery. I became privy to some very interesting information, some of which I would probably just as soon not have known, including how often I would have to get up during the middle of the night in the eighth and ninth month. It was sort of unnerving when I realized that I was beginning to appreciate this rite of passage that I was experiencing.

The typing pool was not the only place where I experienced this familiarity. It seemed to cross sex barriers. The process of giving birth is apparently an aspect of the human condition that is viewed as community property. Men would come up to me and, without giving it a second thought, rub my tummy much as the faithful rub Buddhas in Japan. Being someone who is not at all "huggy-feely," this took some real getting used to. Had the tummy touch occurred on the subway, I would have jumped out of my skin. Since this happened in the office, usually with people I knew, it seemed only odd. Here were businessmen who softened, even if only momentarily, when confronted with the miracle of life that I represented.

Before I began to develop too big a head about my Madonna influence, though, I happened to meet one of my major competitors in the lobby of the United Airlines Red Carpet Club as I was heading back to the east coast the following week.

"Rochelle, the word on the street is that you're going to have a baby."

"The grapevine is absolutely right as usual, Chris."

"Well, I can't tell you how happy this makes me. After years of losing business to you, I now have the satisfaction of knowing that at least once in your life YOU got screwed!"

CHAPTER 4. I HAVEN'T GOT A THING TO WEAR

Dress to impress.

After revealing the fact that I was having a baby and was not a long overdue candidate for Weight Watchers, I could finally go shopping for maternity clothes. This was becoming pretty urgent because the silk shirtwaist dresses which I favored for my regular office attire were getting more than a wee bit snug.

I've always operated on the theory that "when the going gets tough, the tough go shopping." So, as a card carrying member of Shoppers Anonymous, a maternity shopping extravaganza was something I was really looking forward to. As with other of my assumptions about pregnancy up until now, building my next five-months wardrobe would prove to be more challenging than I had originally thought.

When John Molloy's best seller, *Dress For Success*, was the rage a few years back, I read the book and dismissed it as so much nonsense. Instead I continued to favor a softer, silkier, more colorful and feminine look. As a matter of fact, I've never worn the traditional skirted business suits Molloy advocates. At this moment, though, I could have used any clothing consultant, including Molloy, for guidance.

Buying maternity clothes that seemed even remotely suited for someone in an executive position was even more frustrating than I ever could have imagined. For one thing, since the lion's share of pregnant women are not upper management women (just as a majority of working women are not sitting in the corner office), most maternity clothes have not been designed with that level of business appropriateness in mind.

I'm not sure why this surprised me. The fashion industry as a whole has largely ignored the fact that most working women at any level want classic, tasteful attire. They don't necessarily want to wear three piece pinstripe suits to match their male counterparts, but like men, they want clothes that are well made classics that don't go out of style every time Bill Blass sneezes.

Calling Alan from New York one night I told him how frustrated I was. So far, during my brief shopping forays to find maternity clothes that could be worn in a business environment, I had come up with zilch. With typical male insouciance, Alan announced that as soon as I got back to Denver, he would squire me around to all the maternity shops, where in a day he would take charge of completely outfitting me with a more than adequate pregnancy wardrobe.

Because I spent so much time during each week either in my New York City office or on the road cross-country with my sales managers, Alan and I tried to spend as much time together on weekends as possible. Spending an entire day shopping would not make it to the top of Alan's list of favorite things to do, so I was quite impressed that he was actually quite eager to accompany me on this adventure.

As I hugged the receiver and relished the warm fuzzy thoughts I was having about this prince of a fellow I'd been married to for nine years, he continued, "For crying out loud, what's the big deal? You walk in, try on a few things in your size, pay for them and then we go home."

Right.

The next weekend, by the time we had visited every store in Denver that even remotely resembled a maternity outlet, Alan had a migraine and I had no clothes.

We concluded that the maternity industry had never heard of the concept of natural fibers. Even though I thought double knit polyester went out with wide-lapel leisure suits for men, some of the fabrics used for maternity wear looked as though they would ignite at the mere mention of a match and others seemed to have been created for endurance - like the Herculon on my sister's family room couch - rather than style.

Nor had the notion of style seemed to have occurred to this industry. Unless dotted Swiss eyelet ruffles on the puffed sleeves, collars or cuffs of a fuchsia garment fashioned seemingly for Jabba the Hud constitutes style, being chic and pregnant was obviously a contradiction in terms for these manufacturers. Apparently they felt that tent-like apparel designed by Omar and produced in a spectrum of garish (or worse, uninspired) colors was totally acceptable. I wanted something designed by Gucci, or Liz Claiborne, or Ralph Lauren, or anybody with some imagination and class. I wanted . . . to scream.

Having struck out in Denver what a stroke of luck it was for me, when on my next week's trip to New York, I got an unexpected phone call from the chairman of the board of our firm, Sig Zises. Sig's most recent wife, Judy, was making quite a name for herself (and a bundle of money in the process) as the founder and president of "Sweet Mama," designer of haute couture for the affluent pregnant.

"Rochelle, clear your calendar for the rest of the day. I'd like to do something special for you."

Now the last time Sig did something special for me it involved two tickets to a fund raiser for his favorite charity that only set me back $1,000.

"I've worked out with Judy to meet you at her showroom. Her fall collection is just out and she'll squeeze you in between buyers today so that you can pick out a few things for yourself."

"Thanks, Sig. That's really swell of you. I'll cancel my afternoon meeting. Be ready in fifteen minutes."

Not knowing exactly what to expect, I followed directions. When the chairman of the board calls, I respond.

Things started out really well. Sig had ordered a stretch limo (not an uncommon taxi alternative in the Big Apple) which was waiting for me on Third Avenue. The driver whisked me through Manhattan to Fifty-seventh Street in the famous garment district. We stopped in front of a nondescript brownstone.

Four flights up a dim stairwell, I was warmly met by Judy who grabbed my arm, steered me through the door and into the combination showroom-headquarters where I was greeted by her mother and racks and racks of a designer-line of maternity wear.

"Rochelle, you must let me show you our new line."

For all my external symbols of worldliness and sophistication, inside I was still that hick kid from Kenora. What the heck was a "line"? I thought that was a come on that some guy used in the back seat of a 1976 Chevrolet just before he tried to take advantage of your virginity. I was about to find out that I wasn't exactly wrong.

I'll hand it to Judy. She had been astute enough to identify an unfilled need when she saw one. Recognizing that even high society women have babies, and that there was definitely a shortage of well designed and carefully constructed clothes for them, she had carved out a niche at the upper end of the market. Her designs were carried by Saks and Neiman Marcus, not K-Mart and Sears. Now this was going to be more like it.

I quickly discovered that all the glamour of the garment industry must be reserved for Vogue magazine. When you go to a designer's showroom, the inner sanctum of fashion for department store buyers, dressing rooms are not part of the architecture. I soon found myself, belly protruding several inches, standing in my underwear in the middle of a huge drab colored, cement floored auditorium with Sig's very Jewish mother-in-law, Phoebe, who was putting me into one ensemble after another cooing, "Maahvahlous, daahling . . . simply maahvahlous . . . this is really YOU."

I had absolutely no idea if this was really ME or not because in addition to no dressing rooms, there was not a mirror in sight. I was also becoming very uncomfortable and increasingly nervous with the whole process. There wasn't a price tag on anything that I had tried on. Were you supposed to ask or in the designer biz was that considered the height of insult?

Did I dare offend the chairman of the board's wife and mother-in-law with the admission that I wasn't all that crazy about any of the outfits no matter how maahvahlous, especially the fire engine red with black polka dot dress? Even without benefit of mirror, I had a feeling that as I progressed in girth, this garment could make me resemble a watermelon on legs.

Surely male executives are not tortured by such indecision or lack of initiative when they are ordering custom made suits on Seville Row, in Hong Kong or whatever. Not wanting to appear gauche, cheap or rude, and thinking to myself, "Now what would Harold Geneen (one of my business heroes) do?" another executive decision seemed in order. I would neither ask about price or express my opinion about the ensembles; I would be a first class chicken instead.

With what I hoped was a smile plastered on my face, I thanked Judy and company lavishly for their time and talent, gushed profusely over everything they had shown me and then, making an exaggerated glance at my watch, announced that if I didn't leave now that I would be late for an extremely important appointment. That wasn't entirely a falsehood. To save my ravaged nerves, I desperately needed an appointment with Le Bubble Bath.

As outfit after outfit went into the bags and with me having no idea how much I was spending or how any of these things looked on me, I agonized that I would have to take out a second mortgage on my home to pay for Sig's "treat." As luck would have it, only a small home equity loan was needed to finance the six shopping bags I walked out with.

When I finally got back to the hotel I immediately started to run the water for the bubble bath. As the tub filled and the smell of the bath salts began to waft through the room, the next thing I did was run to the bedroom, try each ensemble on one by one and, looking long and hard in the full length mirror, make a damage assessment. Twenty minutes later as I lay lounging in the warmth of the tub, I reasoned that, with only five of the outfits being total disasters, this afternoon could have been worse, much much worse.

Following my trip to "Sweet Mama," I was still on the quest for maternity clothes that would be smart, comfortable and businesslike.

As I continued to commute back and forth from Denver to New York for business with my midsection reaching crisis proportions, I started to lead a double life. Business executive by day, shopping crazed pregnant woman by night. I scoured the city for good looking, stylish dresses. While scanning the MART section of the *Wall Street Journal* one day, I stopped casually flipping to the next page when I eyed a small display ad that seemed to be the answer to my prayers. A mail order company that catered to the maternity clothing needs of executive women was offering a free catalog and they even had an 800 number.

Of course, why hadn't I thought of this before? Direct mail and catalog shopping were the latest marketing trends for busy consumers. Undoubtedly they realized the market that existed for women such as myself. My fingers quivered slightly as I dialed the toll-free number, but my voice was confident when I gave the customer service representative my name and address so that she could send me the latest catalog.

Each day as I shuffled through the day's mail, I eagerly looked for THE all important maternity catalog. Within a week it had arrived. The front cover boldly proclaimed executive maternity wear. But there had to be a mistake. Where was the executive attire? The four color photos revealed nineteen year old, rake-thin models sporting cutesy navy blue empire waisted polyester frocks with crisp dotted Swiss lace ruffles on the sleeves.

Desperately I turned the pages, sure that on the next page the sophisticated "designer" dresses that I needed would be found. Reaching the last page, I realized that this was not the case. How, I asked, can they call these executive dresses? In what way are they businesslike? They were exactly like all the dresses I had seen in Denver and rejected as totally inappropriate for my needs. Wait a minute. Not exactly. As I slowly flipped the pages again I realized that the "value added" by the manufacturer to qualify these as "executive" dresses was the little floppy bow tie that had been tacked to the neck of each and every one.

My frustration about finding clothes that would somehow help me maintain some semblance of an executive image for the next few months was something that I commiserated about with all my female friends, co-workers, acquaintances and any strangers who would listen at length. Most just nodded sympathetically. One, however, had an inspiration.

When I was eight-months pregnant, one friend suggested, "Why don't you have some dresses tailored for you?"

How obvious. Boy, what an oversight on my part. This was a wonderful idea. However, by this time the satisfaction that I would feel by buying custom made silk dresses that I could only wear for at the most four weeks longer simply did not justify the expense. So, I continued to wear my "Sweet Mama" threads right up to the end - fire engine red with black polka dots and all.

(Five years later, my current secretary announced her first pregnancy and opted for the custom couture route. A stunning, six foot tall brunette, she created her entire maternity wardrobe with Vogue patterns and the talents of a terrific seamstress. The effect was classic, business like, professional and ... smashing."

Finding most of the other garments that I needed during pregnancy was relatively trouble free. There was just one tiny little hitch with one tiny little item of apparel - pantyhose.

In college my friends and I agreed that pantyhose were the most brilliantly created garment ever designed for women. Pantyhose freed us from garter belts that sagged and popped, girdles that threatened to inhibit all circulation from the waist down, and garters that dug into our thighs all day and left welts all night until we got up again the next morning and it started all over again.

I was almost ready to suggest to the Pope that the inventor of pantyhose, whoever that divine person may be, be nominated for sainthood. That blessed person had delivered all womanhood from the tyranny of hose and garter forever. You can talk about Neil Armstrong's "one small step for man" on the moon all you want. Pantyhose were a giant step forward for womankind.

That was my philosophy before I was eight months pregnant.

Up until then, by adjusting sizes and models, my regular brand of pantyhose had been just fine. After two and a half months I bought the next bigger size; at four and a half months I advanced to queen size; at six and a half months I purchased the maternity model, but at eight months I was in trouble - big trouble.

At this stage I absolutely could not find a brand or size of pantyhose manufactured anywhere in the free world that even remotely fit. They either bagged around my knees like inner tubes or were so tight around my stomach that I feared the baby would be in danger of asphyxiation or developed runs in the crotch because of so much tension that no amount of clear nail polish would remedy - and I couldn't see where to apply the polish anymore anyway! The one day I tried to repair a run, I painted the polish on liberally where I thought the longest tears were only to find that when it dried my thighs had glued themselves together. Thank God, I didn't use Super Glue!

And it wasn't just the fact that the pantyhose didn't fit. I could no longer bend over to get them on. Every shred of dignity that I had maintained up until this point as the female executive-who-just-happens-to-be-pregnant was quickly discarded the first morning Alan had to help me get into my pantyhose.

"AAAAAlan, HHEELLPP," I squealed.

"What is it? Did your water break? It's too early for that. What's the matter?" Alan sputtered as he came running out of the bathroom, razor in one hand, shaving cream smeared on half his face.

"I can't get my pantyhose on," I replied, hyperventilating from the effort, as the tears welled up in my eyes.

"Oh, good grief. Is that all?"

"Is that all? It's humiliating. I can't bend over, I can't even get close to my toes."

Waving the unruly pantyhose over my head I continued, "I can't get these blasted things on, and I've got a breakfast meeting in twenty minutes."

"Sit down and give them to me. How hard can this be?"

With me perched on the edge of the bed, Alan wadded one leg of the pantyhose into a ball, shoved it onto my foot and yanked it mid calf. Then he wadded up the other leg and repeated the process.

"There, now you can pull them up the rest of the way." And he was off to the bathroom to finish shaving.

That wasn't so bad, I thought. I probably was over reacting. And with all the energy I could muster, I managed to pull the pantyhose up over my knees and thighs and smooth them on a bit. All went well until I got to the panty part of the hose. I simply couldn't stretch them out enough to get them up and around my greatly increased circumference.

"AAAAAAAlan, HHEELLPP," I shouted.

"My God, now what?"

"I can't get the pants on now."

"Well, just leave them around your crotch."

"Alan, I can't do that, it's like walking with a hobble on. It's hard enough to keep my balance as it is."

"Oh, for heavens sake. This is ridiculous. It never occurred to me that you were going to need personal valet service just to get dressed in the morning. I would have seriously considered the vasectomy if I had known this."

"Alan, get over here NOW or this may be the last child you ever have with me," I bellowed.

Alan grabbed the front waist of the pantyhose and I dug my thumbs into the back. With a 1-2-3 and four jumping jacks we heaved my bulk into the rest of the hose. I would like to tell you that my dear husband was helpful, patient and coordinated enough to adapt gracefully to our new morning routine. The truth is that while this gave us many hearty laughs later, this was not one of his favorite things about my being pregnant.

And frankly I wasn't too thrilled with it either. But how was I to know that the insult of being stuffed into my pantyhose like a knockwurst sausage was to be the least of the indignities in store for me in connection with the delivery of our new little bundle of joy?

CHAPTER 5. THE GAME PLAN

Making the Normandy invasion look easy.

After recovering from the exhaustion of coping with the complexities of clothing my expanding body parts, it occurred to me that I'd better get busy planning for what Baby Wallach would wear . . . and eat . . . and where he/she would sleep . . . and who would nurture him/her in my absence . . . and what about an obstetrician to deliver baby and a pediatrician to oversee baby's care.

Once I got started with this train of thought, my list kept getting longer and longer. This was getting to be just a little more complex than I had originally anticipated, but certainly no more complicated than any of the many multi-faceted business projects that I had successfully tackled over the years.

The cornerstone of whatever success I'd enjoyed in my business ventures over the years had been based on a well constructed and executed business plan. Psychologists tell us that, during times of stress, we revert to our basic patterns of behavior. Well, my basic pattern is to start making lists, develop a written plan (with a capital P) and then to ACT.

I have long been a proponent of the axiom, "People don't plan to fail, they just fail to plan." In fact, I have felt so strongly about the role that planning plays in success in the business world that I even penned an industry best selling book extolling its virtues. Failing to plan is one of the key reasons that people fail in business - as sales people, managers, executives, whatever. Failing to plan had never been one of my problems, and I didn't intend for it to be one now.

Preparing an annual business plan had been part of my pattern for years. Every time I launched a new financial product or initiated a new marketing campaign, I always started with a well conceived game plan. No NFL coach ever worked harder on his plans than I did. So maybe he had to cope with giving those half-time pep talks to a bunch of guys in dirty uniforms who smelled like goats, and I gave motivational speeches to guys in three-piece suits who smelled like Brut, but you get the idea. Our objectives were the same. We both played to win.

How different could having a baby be to launching a new product? After all, you plan for its arrival, give it about nine months to gestate, and then you launch. As a matter of fact, I was currently involved with preparing to launch a new mutual fund family, so it was just natural that I would also develop a plan for introducing Baby Wallach to the world and our lives at the same time.

With pencil poised and yellow tablet in the center of my desk, I pulled open the credenza drawer and extracted the business plan outline I'd relied upon for years. Leaning back in my chair I looked out the window. The sun was shining, little puffy clouds were drifting past the Empire State Building, twenty-two floors below me Manhattan was bustling with activity, and . . . I was dawdling.

I hunkered down over my desk and began to write. Forty-five minutes later after filling in the blanks of my tried and true, standard business plan format, I had penned a rough outline of the principles of parenthood that I believed in at the time (naive though they are in retrospect) and a workable plan for the arrival of our Bundle of Joy emerged:

I. Mission Statement:

> Alan and Rochelle Lamm Wallach (hereafter referred to as "Parents") are committed to maintaining the highest standards of excellence and integrity in the creation, promotion, and delivery of professional parenting services for New Baby Wallach (hereafter referred to as "Baby") so that he/she can achieve his/her full potential as a happy, healthy, well-adjusted, contributing member of society. Once launched the partnership of "Parents" and "Baby" will be known as the "Family."

> In carrying out our mandate, we will be guided by the following values and standards:

> 1. We will conduct ourselves as parents in accordance with the highest standards established by Dr. Spock.

> 2. Parental integrity will be our highest priority. No copping out to whining voices, tearful entreaties, or "all the other kids' moms and dads let them" logic.

> 3. We will strive to achieve economic prosperity to ensure the financial security of the family. This however does not guarantee that Baby

will be presented with a Ferrari upon celebrating his/her sixteenth birthday.

4. We will be empathetic and responsive at all times to whatever the needs of Baby may be. This refers to actual needs only and does not include pierced ears for female Baby before age twenty-one or for male Baby EVER. Nor does this refer to Baby's misguided notion that Frosted Sugar Mini Wheats, Mountain Dew, pizza, and Snickers are the four basic food groups and therefore comprise a balanced diet.

5. Understatement and conservatism will be our posture in our and Baby's appearance. This means we will wear clothes that match, never have a Mohawk haircut, avoid safety pins as earrings and expect the same of Baby.

6. We will at all times convey and maintain our image of professionalism as Parents to establish ourselves as admirable role models for Baby. This may require the secret consumption of large amounts of alcohol, enough Valium to sedate an elephant and/or intensive counseling. Wailing, weeping, gnashing of teeth, and the use of four-letter words in private is acceptable.

7. We will foster self esteem and confidence in Baby. High levels of praise will be heaped on Baby for such achievements as using the potty, looking both ways before crossing the street, playing any musical instrument that does not require electricity and graduating from any institution of higher learning including Hamburger U, beauty college, or chiropractic school.

8. We will make realistic commitments and live up to them. Chaperoning the sixth-grade class on a trip to Six Flags Over San Juan or attending any Grateful Dead concert is not realistic.

9. We will work to maintain a teamwork approach to every task, helping each other without hesitation, with loyalty to our Family foremost. Exceptions may include anything that the Parents deem worthy under the Geneva Convention.

10. In recognition of Baby's importance, all appointments will be kept promptly (unless the chairman of the board calls an emergency board meeting) and all telephone calls returned immediately (unless the substance of the call involves parental permission to buy anything advertised on Saturday morning cartoon shows).

II. Situation Analysis

1. The experience of Parents is limited; however, the desire to excel is high.

2. Millions have marched before us down this route - at least some of them with less native intelligence than we. They have made it, so how hard can it be?

3. At first Baby will weigh only six pounds (highly portable), sleep virtually ninety percent of the time (require only limited parental involvement, allowing time to read all instruction manuals), and eat only natural foods (no cost, since provided by female Parent).

4. Adequate funding exists to hire and train appropriate support personnel.

III. Basic Cost of Doing Business

A. Cost factors:

1. Maternity Wardrobe
2. Obstetrical Services
3. Hospital and Medical Expenses
4. Imported Cigars
5. Pediatric Care
6. Professional Personnel
   - Nanny
   - Tutors
   - Family Therapist
   - Career Counselor
   - Personal Trainer
7. Diaper Service
8. Food, Shelter, Clothing
9. Professional Fees:
   - PTA
   - Brownie-Girl Scout/Cub-Boy Scout Dues
   - Columbia Record Club
10. Educational and Training Fees
    - Kinder-Care
    - Piano, Swimming and Spanish lessons
    - Montessori
    - Summer Camp
    - Prep School
    - Basketball Camp
    - Reform School
    - Music Camp
    - College
    - MBA/PhD/MD/LLB/JD/MRS/ETC
11. Travel and Entertainment
    - School Bus
    - Big Wheel
    - Clown (for birthday party)

Bicycle
Magician (for birthday party)
Drivers License Fee
Transfusion (for male Parent who goes into
shock when auto insurance increases)
Motorcycle
Rental car (for attending Grateful Dead
concert)
Prom
Air Fare (to college campus)
Air Fare (from campus to home for holidays
during school vacations)

B. Estimated Total Cost of Baby Wallach

1. Total cost of bringing up baby is anticipated to exceed the national debt.
2. Funding sources will be inadequate to cover cash flow.
3. Using U.S. government as a model, deficit financing is suggested.

III. Short-Term Objectives, Goals, and Strategies

1. Determine sex of Baby. This will assure that all clothing and accessories are properly requisitioned and will eliminate the ambiguous yellow/mint-green color scheme.

2. Interview and hire nanny. Coordinate start date with expected Bundle of Joy launch date.

3. Purchase all necessary Baby equipment and furniture.

4. Call interior designer to create proper Baby environment.

5. Choose OB-GYN. Requirement is for someone who graduated at the top of the medical school class, is highly committed to the notion of pain-free delivery through the extensive use of state of the art drug therapy, is warm and sensitive, always has time for the female Parent, and will appreciate the fact that - the immaculate conception not withstanding - this is the most important pregnancy in recorded history.

6. Complete and mail application to socially correct kindergarten.

7. Interview pediatricians. Poll friends for names of most enlightened. Ideal candidate will be caring and concerned about Baby's health and well being but will also totally support Parents' bumbling efforts with the patience of Job.

8. Purchase most recent edition of Dr. Spock. Outline reading schedule for both Parents.

9. Eat healthy food. Avoid like the plague all coffee, Cokes, and sugar substitutes. Anything that remotely resembles alcohol is strictly verboten, including vanilla extract and cooking sherry.

10. Deliver Baby.

11. Bond with Baby.

12. Delegate responsibility to nanny and return to office within two weeks.

13. Raise Baby. Schedule Baby activities on Day-Timer.

With a great sense of accomplishment, I placed the Bundle of Joy Launch Plan in its own manila folder and placed it in my brief case. This was a good plan - comprehensive, well thought out. With this plan as my guide, this whole baby thing was going to be a piece of cake.

It seemed to me that item III.5 needed some immediate attention. The choice of my OB was critical. While I adored my general practitioner, Kerry Higgins, as a thirty-seven year old "primagravida," I knew that even though I was healthy as a horse, I met all the criteria to be classified as a high risk pregnancy and ought to seek out a board certified OB.

The Gottesfeld brothers were probably the best known OB-GYN team in Denver. They also had one of the busiest practices in town. I really did want and need someone who was every bit as highly skilled and respected as they, but someone who had not been discovered yet, someone whose practice was not on the level of General Motors, someone who would have lots of time for personal attention.

Because I had waited so long to start a family, I viewed this pregnancy as very special (OK, it wasn't the Immaculate Conception or anything, but I felt like it at least ranked up there with Barbara Bush's pregnant Presidential pup or something), and I wanted a doctor who would share this vision with me. On the recommendation of several friends, I finally called and made an appointment with Dr. Blake Martin-Mills. I figured the hyphenated last name was a good sign. This must be a pretty with-it doctor. Not one of those stuffy, conservative types.

I began to have doubts about my decision during the first few minutes of my first appointment. As I sat in his waiting room wearing my "Sweet Mama" original, I looked around the room at the other expectant moms. This was an earthy crowd to describe it mildly. Next to me was a young woman with long straight hair wearing a tie-dyed muumuu of sorts. With Green Peace buttons on her collar proclaiming "Save The Whales" and "Recycle: It's The Right Thing To Do," she reminded me of a 1960s hippy. Maybe she got caught in a time warp. But if so, she wasn't the only one.

The gal sitting directly across the room, who was about to deliver any day now, was apparently not acquainted with either Nair, waxing, or the concept of smoothly shaven legs. Dark, coarse hair, long enough to knit, fuzzed down her shins and curled around her ankles. She had her daughter with her, a youngster who I guessed to be about four-years old, quietly playing with the puzzles in the corner. Probably a very nice woman, I told myself, who raises very well adjusted children. Really, I must not be such a snob.

Just then the daughter sauntered over to her mother and announced, "Snack, Mommy, snack." Expecting the mother to hand her a Ziplok bag filled with Cheerios or a box of raisins, I was absolutely floored when the mother unbuttoned her blouse, the little girl climbed on her lap and began to nurse.

On the other side of this maternal version of a vending machine was a gal who by this point was looking well dressed to me - actually a possible candidate for a fashion magazine - in blue jeans with shredded knees sporting a bright pink T-shirt which was a little snug across her tummy. The shirt was emblazoned with BABY on the chest and below the inscription was an arrow pointing boldly at her protruding middle. I definitely felt overdressed.

I had arrived a little early for my appointment, and since I had already critiqued the waiting room crowd, I looked around for something to read until the nurse called my name. The magazine rack was filled with a collection of publications, only one of which I even recognized (*Rolling Stone*); the others I had never seen before - *Vegetarian Cooking, Zen Mother, Babies . . . Naturally, Mother Earth Catalog.*

Not finding any *Time* or *People* magazines filled with shallow mindless articles to flip through, I looked on the end tables. More unusual reading material abounded - pamphlets on *Birthing Your Child in a Shallow Stream, The Beauty of Natural Childbirth, Bee Pollen and Your Baby, Diapers and Composting the Easy Way, Choosing A Midwife* - books with titles like *Having Your Baby at Home, Infant Massage, Vegetarian Mother and Baby Cookbook, Midwife's Guide to Pregnancy, No Fault Toilet Training* - and finally a cassette tape titled "Womb Sounds."

The nurse finally called my name just as I was wondering what Henry Mancini would have thought of the musical value of the womb sounds tape and ushered me into the examination room. After unrobing and donning the obligatory no shape, no style, scratchy examination gown - gosh, where is Bill Blass when you need him - I stretched out on the table and found myself gazing up at a mobile of dolphins mounted overhead (so much the better to hypnotize you while you are being poked and prodded). The rough brown paper on the examination table was prominently labeled "Recycled, Biodegradable" and was testament to the fact that natural was the watchword of this office.

Dr. Martin-Mills was a pleasant young man who wore plaid shirts, hiking boots and John Denver wire-rimmed glasses. As he went through his routine, he kept asking questions about how much bran did I eat and did I meditate once or twice a day. I began to get the very uneasy feeling that he was not going to take kindly to my "knock me out and wake me when it's over" philosophy of birthing. He really wanted me to EXPERIENCE this.

The clincher occurred during the consultation in his office. I noticed a back pack under Dr. Martin-Mills desk. Never the Euell Gibbons type, I was now firmly convinced that this guy was not only a proponent of nuts, berries, and GrapeNuts as well as natural childbirth but that he may even have been the author of the *Birthing Your Child in a Shallow Stream* pamphlet as well. I did stick with Dr. Martin-Mills for a while. Ever the optimist, I thought I might be

55

able to persuade him that I was either too old for natural childbirth or too much of a coward. These arguments had no effect whatsoever. His mind was as made up as mine.

The final circumstance which signaled the end of our relationship was the fact that whenever I went for my appointment, the receptionist would invariably say, "What are we seeing you for?" My girth would have been the first clue that I didn't need a pap smear. In the two or three months that I stuck it out with Dr. Martin-Mills' office, she never did have a clue as to the reason for my being there.

So much for Dr. Martin-Mills. At the beginning of my fourth month, Stuart and Ray Gottesfeld were called in from the bullpen and took over. They continued to be as busy as ever, but they were both wonderful; their receptionists always knew why I was there, and they did an admirable job as "relief doctors."

The next item to be considered was III.1. Determine Sex of Baby. As it turned out, this was a by-product of the amniocentesis that Alan and I had decided upon as a necessary procedure for my pregnancy. As an older mom-to-be, I wanted to make sure that all was well, so with Alan and my sixteen-week-old fetus in tow, I presented myself at the hospital.

Friends had warned me that having an amnio was pretty grueling - even worse than having a proctoscopy, a thought that instilled instant terror in me - so I will admit that I was a tad nervous about this.

"Mrs. Wallach, come on in." This was the crisply dressed prenatal nurse speaking. "The hospital has prepared a film about amniocentesis for you to see before we start the procedure."

Uh huh. Just like seeing the cartoon before the feature starts, I'll bet.

"You'll see that amnio is really not a painful procedure at all. It's only slightly more complicated than a blood test, so just forget anything your friends may have told you."

This sounded like propaganda to me. I knew my friends. Them I could trust. I didn't know these folks.

Obviously I wasn't the only female who had some anxieties about participating in this medical procedure. So, in an attempt to calm the nerves of new moms such as myself, the hospital had prepared a film all about the process. Viewing the film was meant to allay my fears; however, as the credits rolled, I was far from convinced that this was merely a routine procedure and clearly could not be as simple as a blood test. For one thing, they don't make films about routine procedures because they are in fact just that - routine. The fact that they had produced this film at all only served to make me more suspicious, not less.

After being clothed in another drab hospital gown - I was getting much too well acquainted with these garments and had already decided to suggest to "Sweet Mama" that they come up with a chic number for upscale hospitals - the nurse ushered me into the procedure room whose size and personnel count only served to increase my anxiety. This place was not a warm, cozy examining room. This was at least the size of an operating theater, and it was full of high tech equipment and the people to operate it. In addition to the doctor (a female, by the way), there were two nurses, an intern, and a sonogram technician - appearing to be virtually a cast of thousands to this agitated observer. There were instruments everywhere, but the one that really caught my eye was the fourteen-inch syringe that lay near the doctor's right hand. It looked like a diabetic elephant could have used it.

The whole idea of the amniocentesis, for the uninitiated, is to draw a sample of amniotic fluid from the womb for analysis. For babies of mothers of my age birth defects are more common, and the results of the amnio can detect possible

57

problems. While the principle is not unlike drawing a blood sample for analysis, the actual fact is that the needle had to penetrate the several layers of muscles and tissue of my abdomen as well as the uterine wall to reach the fluid in question. Of course, the trick is to do all this without pricking the baby in the process.

As I surveyed the room, the equipment, and the medical personnel, I felt my blood pressure rising and the muscles on the back of my neck start to tense. I decided that, as soon as I had lain on the examining table, I would close my eyes so as not to witness any of the medical mumbo jumbo that was about to transpire. Operating on the principle that what you don't know (or can't see) can't hurt you, I reasoned that this approach would be less stressful than viewing the realities.

As I was lying on the examining table, all psyched for the ordeal to follow, I felt some cold, gooey jelly being smeared on my tummy. This, I heard the nurse say, was for the ultrasound - which is the "picture" they were about to take of my innards, so they could see the location of the baby. This way they could avoid jabbing him/her with the elephant needle. As I clinched my fists and squeezed my eyes even tighter, there was a loud snapping explosion. With a sharp intake of breath producing an inhaled "Eek" of sorts, I jumped two inches off the table and shouted, "What was THAT?".

"Relax, Rochelle", the doctor said. "I haven't even started yet. I'm only putting on my rubber gloves. Everything is going to be just fine."

Says you, I thought.

With the needle poised mid-air in one hand (all the better to scare the heck out of you), the doctor then began to tap on my tummy with the other while talking to the baby. As she tapped away with something akin to a rumba beat, I began to feel like one of Ricky Ricardo's conga drums.

58

"Come on, baby, come on. Move over", she kept repeating as an incantation. It sounded a lot like the ballpark chatter you hear at a Yankees game.

She continued coaxing the baby to move over so she could position the needle appropriately. At this point my curiosity got the better of me and I warily opened one eye - the other stayed firmly shut so I would only be half as scared this way - and looked at the ultrasound monitor. And there in living black and white, Baby Wallach, swimming from one side of my uterus to the other, had his first photo op. The other eye flew open, the better to view this event. I totally forgot to be afraid and instead focused on this miraculous bit of life inside me that even at this tender age showed signs of being another Mark Spitz.

As it turned out, the nurse had been right, the amnio was every bit as simple as a blood test. The results were all positive, and to boot I discovered that Baby Wallach was a boy. This was sort of like knowing what all your Christmas presents are before you open them. It sure took the surprise out of hearing, "It's a boy," or "It's a girl," in the delivery room, but it totally eliminated any infant couture gaffes. Now I could buy all blue duds and forget the unisex yellow ones. (This also meant I needed to add another item to section III.1 of the Bundle of Joy Launch Plan - Choose Name For Baby - which had just been simplified by the fact that we only needed to consider boy's names.)

Since the amnio also included complimentary, take home Polaroids of the Ultrasounds, I actually had pictures of David-Andrew Wallach when he was only sixteen-weeks-old. These are probably not ones that I will show to his girl friend when he's seventeen. He sort of looks like an amoeba.

I'm surprised that Olan Mills hasn't gotten a corner on this market yet. They could develop some sort of package deal to track pregnancies: an ultrasound picture every four weeks, complete with vinyl covered album in blue or pink for $69.95, and an optional photo session in the delivery room, either stills or video for $39.95.

Clearly this would be targeted to first-time parents only. Face it, after you've been through the drill, those little amoeba pictures all pretty much look the same.

I knew that item III.2 - Interview and Hire a Nanny - would not be a breeze. I was an old hand at interviewing and hiring professional sales and administrative people, clerical and support staff. So, I knew that the quality of the people you hire and retain can shape the success of your organization more dramatically than virtually any other business element. Hallmark Cards didn't get to be number one by hiring the bottom half of college graduates!

Over the course of my twenty years in business, I'd undertaken prolonged and agonizing personnel searches to ensure that I added "just the right" member to my team. Now hiring the right in house lawyer or chief financial officer for an operation is admittedly an important undertaking, but hiring the right nanny has, in the overall scheme of things, decidedly more critical implications. This employee wouldn't be entrusted with anything as mundane as a corporate balance sheet after all. This employee would be overseeing the day-to-day development, value system, manners and life skills of MY child.

Alan and I drew up a list of job duties and a profile of the ideal candidate thoughtfully and with real care. The "job specs" read something like a cross between Mother Teresa and an apprentice to become the Virgin Mary. More about this later, but suffice it to say that we came awfully close. Kathy Schmidt, who became our beloved nanny for close to five years, was an angel to say the least. Every working mom in America should be so fortunate.

CHAPTER 6. BUSINESS AS USUAL

Mother Nature in the boardroom.

With my OB selected, our hospital of choice lined up, our application accepted for Lamaze classes (don't get me wrong here - I had NO intention of delivering á la natural - I just wanted to understand this whole baby delivery process. I signed up because the curriculum included a two-hour session on anesthesia, and I intended to be drugged to the gills!) and my travel schedule arranged around my prenatal appointments, I gave a sigh of relief. As I crossed those items off of my "To Do" list with a great feeling of accomplishment, I experienced a momentary panic.

I had been enjoying the glow and attention of impending motherhood. I had lost sight (if only briefly) of the fact that I still had a big business to run and a staff who needed some of my time and attention, too. "Get with it, Rochelle," I thought to myself. "Don't lose your edge. You can't go soft now."

And so I focused my attention and energy on conducting business as usual. Initially, there was just one teeny little problem with implementing this sound approach. My body hormones were changing dramatically. This was all well and good as far as meeting Baby Wallach's housing and nourishment needs. However, I felt as though as I had been attacked by a swarm of tsetse flies.

I became absolutely narcoleptic. I wanted to sleep all of the time. I have always been able to survive on very little sleep, so this was totally foreign to me. I slept on airplanes, in the ladies room, in my office, in taxis, and was even known to start to nod off in meetings. I became obsessed with sleep. I would fantasize about sleeping. Park benches even began to look inviting. I would plan where I could next snatch a few winks.

The problem was, a few winks wouldn't do it. I was like an alcoholic on a binge. I didn't want just five minutes to close my eyes; I wanted five hours!! Coffee was not the answer. Caffeine might impair the baby's development. And so I dragged myself through the day.

Friday nights I would board the plane from New York for Denver and be asleep before the stewardess could even coffee-tea-or-milk me. I would sleep through the weekend, board the plane early Monday morning to return to New York, sleep all the way there and stagger out of LaGuardia to hale a taxi to Midtown.

I would doze all the way through the East River tunnel on the way to the office in the back of the cab as the driver, one hand blaring the horn at all times, bounced over pot holes and dodged traffic. The cabbie would wake me as we'd round the corner of Third Avenue and Forty-second Street and pull up in front of my building, so I could pay him. I'd head for the elevator and pray that it wouldn't be too crowded, so I could lean my head against the wall on the way up.

When I was lucky, I would close my eyes in the elevator as I leaned against the brass and smoked glass interior and rest on the way up to the twenty-second floor. A bell-like tone would sound on reaching my floor, the doors would silently part, and I would practically lurch out into the reception area with a glazed look on my face.

"G' Morning, Rochelle," our perky young receptionist, Stephanie, would chirp, "How was the weekend? Did you have a good flight? Here's your mail."

Fortunately Stephanie, while only eighteen, was the oldest of eight kids, so she clearly recognized the look on my face as the result of the new-pregnancy-lack-of-enough-sleep syndrome and not that of someone who's been on a bender all weekend.

I dreaded any meeting that might involve overheads. As soon as they dimmed the lights and the hum of the projector started, I was a goner. This was really humiliating. I had assured Arthur and Jay that this pregnancy would absolutely not interfere with my attention to business (and it didn't during my waking moments), and here I was nodding off at every conceivable opportunity.

I kept calling the Gottesfelds' office asking what I could do, and they kept reassuring me that I would not feel like a participant in a sleep deprivation study for much longer. Well, maybe so but I still needed help. There must have been other women who had successfully coped with this sensation of having overdosed on Dramamine.

I sought the counsel of one of my good friends, a vice-president of our insurance and banking division, who at age forty-one had her first baby. She now had a grueling life-style commuting from her home, husband, and baby in Boston to

New York where she lived during the week. I knew she would have some good ideas.

" Jane, this is Rochelle. Can you talk?"

"Sure. What's up?"

"Jane, you didn't tell me I was going to want to sleep all the time. Even right now while I'm talking to you. I have a total lack of control over my eyelids. It feels as though there are magnets attached to my top and bottom lids that are irretrievably attracted to one another and feel compelled to comply with the laws of physics regardless of the consequences to me. Did this happen to you when you were pregnant with Caroline?"

Jane, a veteran sales manager with over twenty years experience with three well known money management firms, was a dear friend from way back. Caroline was two now. I had not remembered Jane telling me at any time during her pregnancy about the perils of being somnambulistic, but I must be honest and tell you I really hadn't listened much back then.

When Jane was pregnant, if anyone had suggested that I would become a mother anytime during my lifetime, much less within the next thirty months, I would have accused them of either smoking funny weeds or wanting to sabotage my career. So, needless to say, back then I didn't pay much attention or even encourage Jane to talk about it much. Frankly, I'd always steered the conversation back to the stock market anytime Jane began to tell me about the great sale on christening gowns at Bloomies or quickly asked her about her latest sales antics if she started to explain what a saddle block was.

"So you want to sleep all the time, is that it?" Jane was clearly amused.

"Well, that's one of the dangers of letting Alan blow in your ear."

"Jane, I'm serious. This isn't funny. I want to sleep ALL the time. Harvey was not impressed when I dozed off during his economic update yesterday morning. What can I do? What did you do?"

"Well, I did feel a little draggy during the first month or two but honestly that wasn't my biggest problem. I'm probably not the best person to ask. Now if your problem is having morning sickness, I can relate."

"Nope. No morning sickness at all. In fact I'm ravenous all the time. I am supposed to be eating for two aren't I?"

"As long as you remember that you're not eating for two six-foot-two-inch construction workers, you should be OK.

"My biggest barrier to maintaining my professional edge during pregnancy was not sleeping during important policy meetings - although some of those meeting at Citibank and Manny Hanny could have put anyone to sleep. I was overwhelmed with morning sickness. Really, it was the pits. I felt nauseous all the time. The dry crackers theory is a crock. That just made me feel like I was a seasick parrot.

"I'd be in the middle of a heated negotiation and I'd feel like I was on the deck of a rolling ship. I'd be woozy, start to break into a sweat, and feel my tummy want to heave. I can't tell you how hard it is to concentrate when this happens. I'd finish stating my position, ask for a break and dash for the bathroom. It was so degrading. Ross Perot never had to cope with anything so distracting - or disgusting. I never lost any deals because of it, thank God, but I was terrified every time I went into a tough meeting because I never knew when I might be seized with the urge . . . well, you get the idea.

"Sorry, I don't seem to be of much help"

"It's OK, Jane. Thanks anyway. I appreciate the moral support, and I suppose I should be grateful that I'm not also stricken with your malady, but it just seems so darned unfair to me. Getting pregnant was a team effort. Being pregnant is totally one-sided! I'm the one with the big tummy, terminal sleeping disorder, doctor appointments, nanny interviews. Why don't men get to share any of these experiences of perpetuating the human race?"

"Look, Rochelle, you know how guys are. Real big picture. Not so hot with the details. Honey, if men had to have babies, we'd be on the brink of extinction!"

In the beginning of my fifth month, just as Dr. Gottesfeld had predicted, the cloud of tsetse flies lifted, and I was once again my alert self, back to business as usual.

Well, almost.

I've always set the "performance bar" pretty high for the staff and operations I've directed. My expectations as to the amount of effort I find acceptable and the superior results which I have typically established as operating goals have led me to be described by some - but only by folks who don't know me that well - as a dragon lady. So I admit that I have fostered a reputation for myself as a serious, tough businesswoman. While I wasn't crazy about the designation, I must say it was preferable in my estimation to the alternative of being regarded as a "cream puff" or a "shrinking violet." Clearly being wishy-washy, soft or incompetent was not the image I wanted to project.

Well, to my horror I started to notice that I was beginning to be VERY sensitive. I began to mist up over the slightest things. My tear glands were working overtime. Was this related in any way to the fact that my mammary glands were also very active? If the lyrics to that rousing spiritual are true that "the neck bone's connected to the collar bone, the collar bone's connected to the back bone," was it perhaps possible that my tear glands were connected to my

66

mammary glands? If there was any correlation between these two facts, then Baby Wallach was going to be well nourished indeed!

Tears would well up at the most inopportune moments. Face it, it's hard to be perceived as a hard driving Wall Street professional when at a business luncheon you start to snivel upon catching the strains of "The Way We Were" over the Muzak. I would feel the urge to cry during performance appraisals - when giving them, not receiving them. I choked up over the little day to day frustrations or criticisms that are just part and parcel of business life that would normally roll off me like water off a duck's back.

Although I did have to excuse myself more than once and step into the hall for a moment or two to pull myself together, I absolutely would not allow actual tears to flow during any business related activity. My throat would constrict for a few seconds (which seemed like hours) during a heated exchange around the conference table, but my colleagues thought I was making a dramatic pause - pregnant pause might have been more apt.

Tears might well up in my eyes, but through a combined effort of frantically blinking and biting my bottom lip (which probably had my staff convinced that I had an advanced "tic" or that the onset of facial paralysis was imminent), there were never tears rolling down my cheeks from nine to five. When I was on my own time, things were different. Very different. I cried buckets!!

Women in business have been plagued for years by the stereotype that females are overly sensitive and have a predisposition to cry easily. According to men, this predilection has hampered women in their quest to play on the same team with their male counterparts. As if the only thing that women need to do is have their tear ducts permanently removed (would this be a ductectomy?) in order to proceed up the corporate ladder, break through the glass ceiling and land themselves in the executive suite.

Since being in control of my emotions was something I had always prided myself on, coping with these crying episodes was hard. It made me wonder if I would totally fall apart - I didn't - or whether I would ever be tough again - I was. But I'll tell you, I was never very far from a box of Kleenex. Looking back a few years later, after I had relocated to Appleton, Wisconsin, (affectionately referred to as the Paper Valley by the locals due to the large concentration of paper mills in the area), I realized I really should have bought stock back then in Kimberly Clark - the largest employer in Appleton and manufacturer of Kleenex. What a great investment that would have been.

The challenge of conducting business as usual continued.

My work required me to commute from Denver to New York almost every week and to accompany my area sales vice presidents on nationwide broker and customer calls frequently. Having logged 100,000 air travel miles or so annually for years with ease, I really considered myself a seasoned traveler. My billfold full of frequent flyer membership cards gave testament to this fact.

Being a pregnant lady executive gave a whole new meaning to flying the friendly skies. As my body continued to blossom, airline travel became more and more uncomfortable. Just waddling up the aisle to my seat was unsettling. Those aisles seemed to get narrower with every flight. I must have looked like a pregnant pack mule trudging up the aisle with my overflowing briefcase held awkwardly in front, my bulging purse and hanging garment bag slung over my back.

Those little bitty airline seats, that had seemed perfectly adequate pre-pregnancy, now needed a shoehorn to access. Reaching up to put my briefcase into the overhead required the balancing agility normally found only in circus high wire performers. Bending down to place my briefcase under the seat in front of me was no picnic either.

I would finally get settled, much to the relief of the crew and other passengers, and try to get as comfortable as possible. I mean really, how do professional basketball players or Sumo wrestlers do it? They have my sympathy. I was ultimately going to be size eight again. They were always going to be size 48-extra-long or 58XXXLarge.

During the first few months of my pregnancy, as a victim of pregnancy-enduced narcolepsy, I immediately fell asleep as soon as the plane revved up its engines, but later on I was able to get as much work done on flights as I ever had. I've found that being on airplanes provides me with really productive work time - no phone calls, no interruptions. So once settled, I would kick off my shoes and start digging through staff travel expense reports, sales projections, board reports and industry periodicals.

Back then, airline guidelines suggested that pregnant women fly only through their seventh month. Bah, humbug. No way could I stop flying and put my normal modus operandi on hold. Coast-to-coast travel was how my business had to be conducted. So I told little white lies about how pregnant I was and continued my routine of squeezing through the door (where I was eyed by suspicious flight attendants), waddling up the aisle, putting my bag in the overhead, stuffing my briefcase under the seat, plopping down and kicking my shoes off. I wasn't worried a bit. I had seen *The High and The Mighty* and *Airport* and knew that these experienced airline crews could cope with lots more than me going into labor on their flight shift.

I did however underestimate my ability to cope with body bloat. Those pressurized cabins are murder on anyone who is having trouble with fluid retention, someone such as myself who was very pregnant. I have vivid recollections of landing in Denver on more than one occasion and being absolutely unable to get my feet back into my shoes.

The first time this happened, I was headed back to Denver after another week of madcap mayhem in Tinsel Town. That afternoon, I had been highly touched when my staff held the Wall Street executive equivalent of a baby shower for me at that famous New York Central Park eatery, the posh Tavern on the Green. In addition to the many clever gag gifts I received that day, they presented me with a wonderful Teddy Bear all decked out in a pinstripe suit, *Wall Street Journal* tucked under his arm. There being no room in my luggage for the bear, I had carried it onto the plane under my arm.

As we touched down in Denver, I began to collect my paraphernalia and put my shoes back on. Imagine my distress to find they would not slip back on my tender tootsies with ease. Not unlike one of Cinderella's ugly step sisters, I tried to squeeze my toes - now swollen to size eight - into the front part of my size six and a half pumps. Thinking I might be able to smash down the back of the heels and walk on the squashed parts until I could get to the car, I kept trying to prod my feet into the leather but the discomfort brought tears to my eyes.

I waited for everyone else to exit the plane, so there would be fewer witnesses to my undignified departure. Shoving the shoes into my briefcase, which was already merely a thread away from self destruction, I slung my purse and hanging bag over my back and schlepped off in my wrinkled maternity dress and stocking feet, Wall Street bear in tow.

Any young woman who ever harbored the notion that a traveling job was glamorous should have seen me then - rumpled and dishevelled, tired to the bone, sixty extra pounds on my five-foot-two-inch frame, belly protruding, a stuffed bear under one arm and tears streaming down my face. The indignity of the situation was almost overwhelming. Feeling like a little girl whose ice cream cone has just plopped on the sidewalk in front of her, I unceremoniously deplaned. I'm sure that I've looked and felt more pitiful at some other time in my life, but I can't think of when or where.

Alan, upon meeting me at the gate in this sorry state, was appalled.

"You can't walk out of the airport like THAT."

"Are you planning to carry me?"

"Of course not. But you look pathetic. Put your shoes on."

"Alan, I tried but either they were secretly exchanged on the plane with Twiggy's or my feet now belong to one of the Harlem Globe-trotters. I can't get them on - at all."

"Well, maybe if I try to jam them on for you", he responded helpfully.

Murderous glances on my part.

Defensively he continued, "Why on earth did you take your shoes off in the first place?"

Oh, great, a scolding. If I'd had the strength at that moment I would have strangled him.

"Look, I'm sorry, but after hauling this pregnant body around New York all week by the time I get on that 767 I've got to get comfortable. Taking off my shoes is how I do it. How did I know my feet would become the size of hams?"

Looking sorely aggrieved, Alan took my hanging bag and briefcase from me and headed for the parking ramp. Shoes in one hand, Teddy Bear in the other, I traipsed three steps behind him all the way to the car, trying to muster all the dignity I could while reflecting on what a disillusionment I would have been right then to any young woman currently interviewing for a traveling sales position.

Don't do it, honey, no matter how much money they are going to pay you, would have been my advice at the moment. If this is glamour, who needs it?

And who says that women are the weaker sex? Businessmen do not run companies AND have babies at the same time, wear marginally attractive maternity dresses while attempting to muster some semblance of executive bearing, or worry about their feet swelling on airplanes. Victor Kiam, Warren Buffet or Sam Walton would never have gotten themselves in this kind of a fix, I thought. Well, of course not, they didn't have to wear pointy-toed pumps to work. In fact, the late Sam Walton probably never ever wore a pair of wing tips. I'll bet he wore cowboy boots or hiking boots or something equally comfy on his feet. Why couldn't I wear hiking boots? Because they don't come in the shade of green that matches the dress I have on, that's why.

My feet were not all that started retaining fluid. When Valentine's Day came and went and Baby Wallach had requested a late checkout, I began to develop high blood pressure and edema.

Dr. Gottesfeld was adamant, "Get out of your office - NOW. Go home and stay there, with your feet elevated. You need to slow down until that baby decides it's time to be born."

We still had our new funds to launch and only two weeks to go. This was one of the most crucial times of our marketing calendar. The first few weeks of a new mutual fund's existence can be critical to its long-term success. There were dozens of details to choreograph so that we would have a successful roll-out and effective sales kick-off.

Dr. Gottesfeld said I needed rest. I interpreted this to mean that I had to cut back on my 60 hour work week, get my feet propped up on a chair, stay home and not go into the office, not that my business life had to come to a screeching halt. So as soon as I drove myself back home, I called my secretary.

"Teresa, we have a small complication. Apparently my blood pressure is a little out of kilter; I have a little fluid build up and the doctor says I'm banned from the office until I've had this baby."

"So what are you going to do?"

"We've got too much to do and are too close to kicking off the new funds for me to bow out now. I need you to make a few arrangements, so that I can set up an office at home. I sure hope I like this baby because he is really fouling up the works right now.

"Get a phone line installed here at the house, and make sure you can forward my office calls here. Bring me the product roll out files..."

"ALL the files?"

We had accumulated enough paperwork in the course of this project to fill a presidential library. I can't believe all the trees that gave their lives so that we could add three new mutual funds to our portfolio.

"Yes, all of them, then you just plan on coming by the house twice a day with the mail. That way we can keep this ball rolling. Really, Teresa, it won't be that different from the way we conduct business when I'm on the road."

Right. Except that I would be doing it in my living room.

So the business line was installed and both it and my residence phone rang at all hours of the day and night with calls from attorneys, my sales VPs, portfolio managers, our back office and customer service staff, plus aluminum siding salesmen. No wonder people go to an office to work. Where else can you escape from "The Dating Game", "Guiding Light", and water softener sales pitches?

Teresa trekked over faithfully twice a day and we were able to approve the final promotional materials and ad copy, comply with all the Securities and Exchange Commission comments on our offering, and meet all the necessary print schedules. The show must go on was my motto.

It never occurred to me that it might have been acceptable, or even smart, to give myself a period of time to unwind from work and get ready for D(delivery)-day. I was too committed to this image of myself as no mere mortal woman but rather a goddess-super-heroine hewn from granite that could not just have it all, but could DO it all.

Also there was this overwhelming pride in carrying through on my rash statements that having this baby would not interfere with business at all. So martyr that I was, I persevered. Nobody would ever call me a wimp - lots of other things probably - but never a wimp.

Fourteen days after setting up base camp at home, my doctor was ready to get a court order to have me hospitalized. Instead, Alan called my mother who flew in from Winnipeg, Canada, looked me right in the eye and spoke only one word, "BED!" And off I went.

But not without my phones, Dictaphone, and Teresa's twice daily visits.

The original plan was for the new mutual fund to be launched just before the baby's arrival. Then I would have the baby. My back office and administrative staff and sales managers would handle the details of our cross-country training and sales kick-off events, would start calling on all the major brokers, and in two weeks I would be back in the office to take over at the helm.

Once again . . . wrong . . . wrong . . . WRONG.

First the regulatory process bogged down with red tape and approval for the funds were delayed. Each day we waited for approval; each day I got closer to delivery. I knew that the Securities and Exchange Commission had minds of their own and worked at a pace that made Galapagos turtles look like Salukis, but it seemed to me that your own flesh and blood should be a good bit more accommodating.

I'm a great stickler for schedules so the vagaries of this baby's arrival had not been at all what I expected. How did I know that the due date your doctor gives you is merely a rough approximation of when baby is supposed to arrive, not a cast in concrete arrival time like the Swiss train system by which you can set your watch? In this case the estimate of my due date bore as much resemblance to reality as the estimate the house painter gave me to paint our house the year before bore to his final bill. They were both off by a mile!

Seeing no reason to rush out into the cold, cruel world, even to help his mother get her professional show back on the road, this baby was biding his time. This was not a staff member that was willing to break his/her neck to meet a deadline. This was a baby that was just hanging out and obviously very comfortable with his current home.

This should have been a sign to me that this was going to be one independent child.

At long last David-Andrew Wallach and the Whiz Bang Best Little Mutual Fund Family in the World were born within twenty-four hours of one another, neither one on time, and believe me there were some fleeting moments in those first few days when I wondered if either one of them was worth it.

CHAPTER 7. TRUE GRIT

Why do you think they call it LABOR?

As my blood pressure skyrocketed and the fluid retention bloated my body until I resembled an inflatable doll, Dr. Gottesfeld began to introduce the notion of inducing labor. As it turned out, he didn't need to. The Securities and Exchange Commission approved our new mutual fund family on March first, and I immediately went into labor, thus starting the process of making our expanded family a reality on the same day!

There is probably some risk in revealing this fact since the Securities and Exchange Commission may want to send me a bill even this long after delivery for services rendered in inducing labor. With the U.S. budget deficit burgeoning to over $200 billion, U.S. government agencies will undoubtedly stoop to anything to generate revenue.

They say that today's older, more educated women are the best prepared mothers in history. You would think that having paid rapt attention to every itty bitty detail imparted by our Lamaze instructor, plus having spent $200-300 to add every pregnancy preparation and motherhood how-to handbook that's been published in the last two decades to my library, I would have had an inkling about what to expect when labor set in. Not a chance!

The books enthusiastically describe how to monitor the progression of labor until contractions are coming two minutes apart at which time you are advised to telephone your doctor. Most of the relaxation exercises and distractions which are suggested come across as something between a Sunday afternoon picnic and an excursion to the beach. These people should be sued for false advertising - or worse!

Well, I was never completely duped. I guess I did have an inkling that the howling and bellowing that transpired during the birthing scenes featured on the "Dr. Kildare" and "Ben Casey" television series I'd witnessed as a teenager were not entirely for dramatic effect. So, I had absolutely no intention of sucking on ice cubes - how was a numb mouth going to relieve the pain in my abdomen? - or doing chin ups at home - are you kidding? - or self hypnotizing myself to picture myself floating on clouds (right! especially when instead it felt like I was lying on a bed of nails) - when I could be numb from the neck down through the wonders of epidural anaesthesia. I'd made it abundantly clear to Dr. Gottesfeld that there were no heroes in my household, and I wanted a Jewish delivery all the way - wake me when the hairdresser comes!

Interfaith marriages do this to you - your view of life is broadened considerably. In addition to all my Catholic girls' school values, I now had incorporated much of my mother-in-law's philosophy as well. And I'll tell you it wasn't all bad. Face it, being a Jewish-American princess has its moments. My sister-in-law's favorite thing to make for dinner is reservations, and I have a Jewish friend in New York whose idea of the perfect house is 4,000 square feet, no kitchen!

While men belong to "the good-old-boys network" and "secret societies" and fraternities where they purportedly share all the secrets of life, women seem to have nothing comparable when it comes to "'fessing up" about labor. Throughout my pregnancy I'd heard adjectives to describe the birthing experience in glowing terms: wonderful, fabulous, unbelievable, exciting, a thrill. What I didn't hear was the truth. Where were all my close confidantes who could have whispered in my ear, "It hurts like Hell"?

And a pox on all the books that tell you labor pains are just like intense menstrual cramps. Hogwash. Comparing labor pain to cramps is like comparing Lake Superior to the lagoon in Central Park. They are both bodies of water, but at that point all similarity ends.

Notwithstanding the fact that I had paid closer attention to the information delivered during our dozen or so Lamaze classes than I had in any of my graduate level finance courses, I had never been in labor before, and I wasn't really sure I was when it actually began. I just seemed to be experiencing a mild backache. I was not deceived for long, however. When my water broke and the contractions began to register 6.5 on the Richter scale I knew - this was it. Good grief.

I was at least grateful that my water had broken at home. Thinking back later, I always wondered what would have happened if I'd worked right up to the last minute, and my membranes had ruptured during one of my public speaking engagements in front of 250 people. Every public speaking class, book, and audiotape warn you to never allow yourself to be distracted by little gaffes that you may commit on stage like bumping into the podium, dropping a prop, or stumbling as you walk across the stage. Somehow I think that having amniotic fluid suddenly gush out all over the stage would have been the ultimate test of my stage presence and poise.

I had NO idea that even the very short, controlled labor that I planned to have would be like this. I thought labor just meant hard work and I don't mind a little hard work. Actually I don't even mind a lot of hard work. In fact, I thrive on it. I do mind PAIN.

My mother, who had borne five daughters, did intimate once that there was admittedly a little discomfort with childbirth. But what did she know? She was delivering babies during the era when mothers were completely anesthetized with ether, and after the first cramp were sent off to La La Land where they and the baby, who also received a pretty good whiff of drugs, remained in a heavily drug induced state for three days after delivery. According to Mom, she had a couple of labor pains, went to sleep, and three days later woke to find a sweet, clean baby being placed in her arms. Now, in my generation of gung ho mothers, two hours after suffering through the agonies of natural childbirth, the modern woman is expected to start running laps around the maternity ward and lifting weights. This does not strike me as an advance in medical science.

I've always believed in the power of delegation in both my professional and personal life and have throughout my career hired strong, highly capable experienced support staff to do what they do best, so that I can concentrate on doing what I do best. Labor did not seem like one of those things that I could do best. If you can hire nannies and wet nurses, why can't you hire a surrogate birthing staff? If the details can be worked out, maybe this is an idea whose time has come.

I have to tell you that as I was experiencing these contractions that I was not feeling very charitable toward the male gender. Guys were great when it came to being involved with the creation of babies, but where were they when you really needed them? Oh sure, when it finally came time to have the baby, they could hold your hand, and offer encouragement like "you can do it" - much like boxing managers who motivate their badly mangled fighters to hustle back into the ring and take a few more body blows and upper cuts to the jaw while they stay comfortably at the sidelines in the corner - but what you really wanted was for them to FEEL some of this pain.

I was beginning to feel some serious hostility toward this man who was carrying my overnight bag to the car and began to fantasize about schemes to inflict appropriate revenge later. With me doubled over in the driveway during the next contraction, I looked up at Alan, who was placing my bag in the trunk, and I made a solemn vow that if I lived through this, we would never share the same bed again.

As Alan drove me to the hospital, I began to hallucinate and had the most vivid mental picture of Alan and I assuming the characters that Meryl Streep and Jack Nicholson had played in the movie *Heartburn*. In the hallucination Alan turns to me with a concerned, but supportive, look on his face and says, "Honey, you can do it!" To which I respond, "Can't we get someone else to do it?"

After checking in at the hospital front desk (which at that moment resembled to my pain-clouded mind a replica of the front desk at the Bates Hotel), I was shown to a closet called a labor room. For this, insurance companies ante up to $300 a day?

There I was draped in another one of those dreary, open at the back, threadbare hospital gowns. Granted, by now I knew that this was the accepted apparel when one assumed the patient role. But somehow, I thought that for this biggest of all occasions they could have come up with a costume that had some class, some dignity, something that looked . . . well . . smashing.

As my own comfy pajamas were hung on the hook behind the door, I reluctantly donned the horrible, scratchy cotton-poly garment handed me by the nurse. I felt like Scarlett O'Hara discarding her ball gown to put on overalls and work in the fields. How can someone do her best work when she looks like this?

The nurse plumped the pillows, told me to get comfortable (who was she kidding?), and said Dr. Gottesfeld would be in soon.

"Soon? Soon? How soon? Five minutes?

"Say, Nurse, I'm the one who signed up for the pain free delivery. I even called ahead to make sure the drugs were hooked up. What does it take to get this show on the road? I'll pay extra if that's what you need. Money is no object here!"

I was used to "paying up" for scalper's tickets to ensure front row seats at Broadway plays and was sure that the principle of graft could work here, too. Unfortunately, this appeal fell on deaf ears.

"Oh now, Mrs. Wallach, you'll be fine. Doctor has two other women in labor, and he'll look in on you within the hour."

Look in on me? That's not what I had in mind at all. I'd experienced at least a dozen labor pains already. I figured I'd legitimately bonded with the female species. Surely this qualified as going through the rites of passage to womanhood, albeit fifteen years later than my contemporaries.   Remember the commercial, "Try it, you'll like it"? Well, I'd tried it, and I didn't like it - not one little bit. I'd experienced all that labor had to offer. I could tell my own little child birth horror stories now, "Dahling, really, it was excruciating. Just like trying to push a watermelon through your nostril!" and frankly I was finished with being a heroine.

Within the hour! I would be in agony with this watermelon in my nose for at least another hour.

"Alan, I need a distraction from anything remotely connected to having a baby right now. Maybe I could read something. Get me today's *Wall Street Journal*."

"You're nuts. You don't need *The Wall Street Journal*. You need to relax."

"Look, I need a *Wall Street Journal* or I can't relax. According to the nurse, I've got to get through the next sixty minutes before I am eligible for drug relief. I may as well not waste the time just being in excruciating pain. At least I'll feel like I'm accomplishing something productive."

So Alan reluctantly ran to the hospital newsstand and picked up a copy of the *Journal*. As I was finishing page nine, Dr. Gottesfeld came strolling in.

Ray reminded me that since this was my first labor (as though I didn't know this already) and first labors tend to take longer, and since most moms wait out some of their labor at home rather than scurrying in at the first twinge, and since I was dilated less that 1/16th of centimeter, it looked like I would be around for awhile. (Gee, did this mean I should send out change of address notices?) This news made me wish that Alan had also bought *The New York Times*, *The Chicago Tribune*, and the last three issues of *Forbes*. Gottesfeld had just delivered a baby and had another patient in the room next door. He would pop in and see me when he could.

Swell, I was being relegated from center stage to the wings with this guy. I'll bet the doctor with the backpack would have held my hand, recited soothing passages from Kahlil Gibran and wiped my brow for me but it was too late to turn back now.

At 9:00 a.m. the next morning, twelve hours after arriving at the hospital, I was pronounced sufficiently initiated into the rites of womanhood to qualify for drug therapy - at last, I thought - and the epidural was administered.

The beauty of the epidural is that following execution of the procedure, I would feel no more pains from the contractions. The horror of it was how it was administered. The anesthesia is injected directly into the spinal cord - right into the tail bone as it were. After first being hooked up to the contraction monitor, I was instructed to roll over with my knees under my chin (this is not easy to do when you have a seventy-five pound mass protruding between your hips and chest) and my fanny hanging off the side of the bed while half a dozen technicians hovered around. This was decidedly not my most flattering angle.

Concern for my appearance quickly faded, though, as I lay there waiting for the injection when my frenzied brain engaged in exact word-for-word recall of the onerous risks that were spelled out in the written "permission" for this procedure that I had signed when I was admitted the night before. This far from user-friendly document absolved the hospital and all concerned of any liability in the event that the anesthesiologist sneezed or something and as a result punctured my spinal cord in the process of numbing me. Shades of spinal tap!

"Now hold your breath and whatever you do don't move, Mrs. Wallach, don't move even a hair," the anesthesiologist announced.

With knees under my chin, bare buns in the breeze, trying to hold my breath and not move - all this while experiencing another contraction - my reaction to this pronouncement was, "What a choice - paralyzing pain or paralyzed for life." Talk about ambivalence. Always a risk taker, as well as devout coward, I opted to ease the pain and continued.

As the epidural began to take effect, I went numb in all bodily parts south of my armpits. It was fascinating to watch the monitor I was hooked up to register the next contraction and realize that I felt . . . nothing . . . I was floating on a cloud. Now this was what delivering a baby was supposed to be like.

My relief was short lived. After two hours of bliss there was a hitch. My system was apparently very confused at this point and began to exhibit symptoms that were not in my or the baby's best interest - blood pressure rising, clammy hands, breathing problems - that sort of thing. Also, there was a problem with dilation - I wasn't getting anywhere.

Gottesfeld and a platoon of personnel including a respiratory therapist, cardiology technicians and assorted nurses and aides were constantly in and out of the room making it appear like Grand Central Station during rush hour. The decision was to cut back on the epidural - way back - and to start administering Petosin - NOW.

Someday I hope I get to meet the sadists who invented Petosin in their dark little laboratory. It is clearly the most deadly drug that has ever been developed and inflicted on an unwitting public. Sure, sure, it encourages dilation all right. It also causes contractions that can only be compared to being struck by lightning. Rather than contractions that began mildly, providing you with a warning of what was coming so that the Lamaze panting could begin, build to a crescendo and finally subside, these puppies snuck up from behind striking with no advance warning at full force.

Petosin just may be the medical profession's version of Chinese water torture. Next time America is involved in a war and we have prisoners or spies to interrogate, I suggest we just give them a shot of Petosin. They will collapse instantly and spill the beans in minutes. Or perhaps Petosin has already been rejected by the CIA as cruel and unusual punishment in total violation of the Geneva convention so the doctors looked at one another and said, "Well, let's use it on pregnant women instead."

When the Petosin contractions got too bad, the anesthesiologist would inject a little more drug epidurally to start the numbing process all over again, so I found myself drifting between dead weight - the effect you get when you're completely numb - and lightning bolts. During the bouts with epidural I relaxed, finished *The Wall Street Journal* and dozed for a while. When the Petosin kicked in all I could do was grit my teeth and think of new types of revenge to spring on Alan once I was released from this dungeon of torture.

Six or seven hours later, Dr. Gottesfeld had decided that dilation was just not going to happen, that the baby and I were getting exhausted from all the labor and that a Caesarean section was in order.

"Well, fine. Whatever you say. How soon will you do the surgery?"

"They'll be bringing in the gurney in just a few minutes, Rochelle, to take you down to the OR," he replied. "I'll be doing the C-section with the help of the OB resident, so you're going to be in really good hands."

He was interrupted briefly by the appearance of Nurse Smiles Galore who announced that she had come to prep me. A new fear struck me. She, as well as the six or seven technicians who were buzzing in and out of the room from time to time, was going to see me totally naked.

Having viewed the confirmation of my pregnancy call from Kerry Higgins as my permission slip to eat everything in sight, I had proceeded to do just that. Alan, noting early on that I seemed to be waging a nine month campaign to bulk up for sumo wrestling, had established only one hard and fast dietary rule for me to follow, "Never eat anything bigger than yourself at a single sitting," and I had followed it faithfully. Well, come on now. Everyone knows that pregnant moms should have lots of calcium. I just got mine by eating one and a half quarts of Baskin Robbins at a time.

Ignoring Jane's advice entirely, I **had** been eating for two six-foot-two-inch construction workers for the past nine months, and frankly I was suffering from thigh anxiety. I'd been nice and slim before my pregnancy, and now I was not only huge with child, but sporting thunder thighs to boot. To her credit, Nurse Galore never noticed, or at least never commented. After painting me from head to toe with an iodine whose aroma clashed disgustingly with my Estee Lauder, she then proceeded to defoliate me from my waist to my knees. Not only did this prove to be humiliating, in about a week it was itchy as heck to boot.

As she prepped me, she tried to keep the conversational ball rolling. Not knowing that I already knew this child to be a boy (a very stubborn boy who didn't want to be born on schedule, a very inconsiderate boy) she asked a question she'd probably asked a hundred times before, "So what would you like to have Mrs. Wallach, a boy or a girl?"

"Actually, what I think I would like to have most is a seventy-five pound baby," I sighed.

As I lay there waiting for the gurney, I was starting to get a little peeved. For crying out loud, I'd been here for twenty-one hours - twelve of which were in blinding pain - and nine of which I alternated between being struck by either lightning or numbness - and NOW Gottesfeld decides to do the C-section and what's more, he isn't even going to perform it alone - the top, most experienced OB-GYN in Denver needs the help of a resident to get the job done! We could have all saved ourselves a lot of time - and in my case agony - by heading right to the operating room for surgery the minute I came in the door.

Just as the aides appeared in the doorway, ready to transport me down the hall, there was a "crash" call. The whole lot of them raced out to answer the call for an emergency C-section.

Stethoscope around his neck, Ray Gottesfeld turned to Alan, now attired in surgical scrubs so he could witness the arrival of our little Bundle of Joy first hand, and asked, "You hungry? The OR is going to be tied up for at least forty-five minutes. Let's you and I go down to the cafeteria and grab a burger."

As Gottesfeld and Alan headed out the door, Ray turned around and said to one of the nurses, "Say, crank up that Petosin a notch or two and see if Rochelle can make some progress while we're gone."

Grab a burger? Crank up the Petosin? Get someone to help with the C-section? What was I? Chopped liver? These two bozos were going to the cafeteria to stuff their faces with french fries and cheeseburgers while I experienced lightning bolts and waited for the latest trauma to clear out from OR so I could take my place in line. Nothing during this delivery had gone according to MY script!

Burgers, indeed!! I was ready to yank out the epidural and Petosin lines, rip off the contraction monitor, and with my tacky gown flapping open, exposing my ample back side, follow them down the hall with *The Wall Street Journal* under one arm, my pajamas under the other, my purse over my shoulder, car keys in hand, screaming, "That's it. I've changed my mind. I've decided NOT to have a baby after all."

While Ray and Alan dined, I got progressively more anxious and then . . . panic gripped me. I was tired, I was in pain, and I was scared. When Alan came back with the most incredible burger breath I have ever smelled, I was shaking like a leaf and tears were welling up in my eyes.

Alan knew better than to say something comforting and totally useless like, "I know what you're going through." I would have decked him right then and there. He sensed that I was genuinely scared and elected to corral Gottesfeld and pull him into the room to reassure me.

"What's the matter?" he asked.

"I don't want to do this."

"Why not?" asked Gottesfeld, finally displaying some sensitivity.

Tears escaped from my eyes and rolled down my cheeks. Expecting to hear reassurances to the contrary I burbled, "I'm afraid I'm going to die."

With complete seriousness, he smoothed out a spot on the bed, sat down, and took my cold clammy little hands in his warm large ones. With a sad puppy dog look in his eyes, he gazed at me with a totally deadpan expression and said, "Look at it this way, Rochelle. I've lost two on the table this week already. What do you really think the odds are that I can lose another one in the same week? You'll be just fine."

With 40,000 comedians out of work, I had to have an OB who considered himself the Don Rickles of hospital humor. But Ray's comic relief, macabre though it may have been, was exactly what I needed. I cracked up at his totally outrageous premise and off we went to the OR.

Twenty-two hours after crossing the portals of Rose Medical Center, I was finally on my way to deliver this baby. The cast of characters assembled in the OR: Gottesfeld, pediatrician, anesthesiologist, head OB resident, two nurses, Alan. As Gottesfeld poised himself to begin, a nurse ran into the OR and stopped him. There was a serious emergency next door involving a premature delivery with a C-section, and they needed the OB resident ASAP. He scurried out.

Ray, to his credit, knew that my courage at his point was about as fickle as the lion in the *Wizard of Oz*.

"Don't go away. I'll be right back."

So, where would I go? And in five minutes he reappeared with, I swear, a teenager whom he introduced as Harry, the head surgical resident. Get real. Harry wasn't even old enough to shave yet. Had I never met Harry, I would have told you that the whole concept behind the television show, "Doogie Howser, MD", was totally implausible. However, considering Harry, maybe not.

Peering over my belly and between my knees at this pip-squeak swathed in surgical greens, I asked, "So, Harry, how long have you been an obstetrician?"

"Well, actually, my speciality is surgery, Mrs. Wallach, not obstetrics."

At this point Alan, who was standing at my head jumped in, "And what exactly is your speciality?"

"Gallstones."

"But you've done C-sections before?"

"Not really. But Ray here is going to talk me through my part of the procedure, so how hard can it be?"

Terrific. This was going to be just like delivering a huge gallstone for him. I guess this was going to be a very special delivery after all, but certainly not in the way I had originally envisioned.

And so David-Andrew Wallach was born on March 2 at 7:05 p.m., twenty-two hours after the commencement of labor, delivered by Ray, the king of hospital humor (who I found out later writes all his own material), and Harry, the crown prince of gallstones.

David-Andrew Wallach, with his fuzzy sprinkling of bright red hair, was not the tow-headed, pink and white Cupid, Valentine's Day baby I had planned on. But as Nurse Galore put him in my arms for the first time, I knew without a doubt that he was the most perfect manifestation of the Bundle of Joy Business Plan I could have imagined.

In all fairness to Ray, although there were moments when I could have strangled him with the Petosin I.V. tube, I must confess that he was remarkably caring and attentive throughout this whole ordeal. He stayed right with me for over twelve hours (from 7:00 a.m. until after David-Andrew was born) even though his mother was flying in from the east coast for a special visit. Ray had planned to pick his mom up at the airport and take her to a nice restaurant for dinner but instead stayed with me while his wife did the honors. Since devotion to my needs meant that he was late for his own family dinner, Alan and I later presented him with a gift certificate for one of the nice gourmet restaurants in Denver in appreciation for service above and beyond the call of duty.

I never counted on a C-section. It threw a real monkey wrench into the plans I'd had to be up and at 'em ten minutes after delivery. I had told my bosses and staff that I'd be back into the office in two weeks. Now after major gallstone . . . er . . . abdominal surgery I wasn't going to be able to be.

No amount of "grin and bear it" was going to erase the fact that I'd been split stem to stern to spring free David-Andrew. With the rise in C-section births - now about 25% of all deliveries - people seem to have lost sight of the fact that a Caesarean is major surgery. Not only that, it hurts like heck!!

After the surgery, Gottesfeld administered a massive dose of painkiller which not only numbed me but also induced the euphoria women experience after a vaginal delivery. The idea was to make my brain forget that I had been sliced like a watermelon across your lower midsection. This was well and good while it lasted. But the next morning euphoria had faded, and I found myself face to face with reality - severe discomfort - and eye to eye with a former Marine drill sergeant of a nurse who woke me at 6:00 a.m.

A twenty-year veteran of the OB floor, five-foot-eleven and all woman, she addressed me at the top of her lungs as though I were a new boot camp recruit, "Congratulations, Mom. Now up and at 'em. Into the john to get your hair done and put some make up on that pretty little face of yours. When we're done with that we'll start exercising!"

Oh, my God. I hoped she didn't have push-ups in mind. Pre-delivery, whenever the idea of exercise had crossed my mind, I would lie down until the thought passed. My idea of exercise was jogging as far as the bathroom in the morning to brush my teeth and lifting bottles of nail polish during my weekly manicure. Here I was hooked up to an I.V. pole feeling as though I'd been one of the dummies in the Volvo crash commercials, and she wanted me to start training for a triathlon! Spare me. I could barely move and a gal resembling Eileen Brennan in the *Pvt. Benjamin* movie was propping me up in the john and trying to get my eyeliner on straight, so I would look nice for my visitors.

This C-section business was literally a pain! My recovery time was going to be much longer than I had anticipated. It would be six weeks before I would even be allowed to drive a car, let alone get on a plane again and resume my cross-country commuting schedule.

My foot long incision and Gottesfeld's mandate that under threat of death (or worse, having to wear one more hospital gown) I was not to step foot into my office for three weeks was going to be a slight inconvenience. This was definitely going to complicate things a little. No stranger to challenges, I mentally did a quick rewrite of the product and Bundle of Joy business plans and dived back into the fray.

Since we'd received SEC approval to start selling our new funds on March 1st, our nationwide sales and marketing efforts were launched the day David-Andrew was born. I had a conference call with my staff scheduled for March 3 just to make sure that each of their individual efforts were on track. Teresa called to see if I were up to the call or if I wanted to reschedule.

"Don't be silly, Teresa. Even though they won't let me go to the bathroom without help and about seventy-five percent of my body is not fully functional yet, my vocal chords are just fine. Believe me, I can still talk."

And talk I did, the very next day, with my staff of sales and marketing vice-presidents, all at airport phones and offices across the country, and me, flat on my back in the hospital. We had a full forty-five minute conference call. Since this interaction was audio only, I was able to use my voice and choice of words to both praise and cajole, inspire their efforts, pump them up a little, and generally convey my confidence in them with my usual sense of enthusiasm. Thank goodness, the long predicted advent of video-conferencing on every telephone in America has so far been more hype than reality, and no one could see me.

I was hooked up to a spaghetti factory of I.V. tubes, still wearing my drab green hospital gown, hair looking like it had been combed with an eggbeater, phone cradled on my shoulder, pencil tucked behind my ear, sales literature spread out on my lap for reference, nursing my now twelve-hour-old baby. It was bliss. While the vice-presidents and I droned on about sales quotas and strategies, David-Andrew contributed to the conversation via little slurps and gurgles. I was back in the thick of business, only this time with a precious baby at my side. At that moment I was truly convinced that I had it all.

CHAPTER 8. AND BABY MAKES FIVE

Two people, two careers, one baby.

It was a bright sunny Spring morning when, with David-Andrew in my arms, Alan on one side and my mother on the other, I left the safety of the hospital and headed for home. I mentally congratulated myself on how well everything was going so far. The baby and our new funds had both been successfully launched - mostly on schedule.

Granted, the C-section had been an unexpected glitch in what had been for the most part an otherwise almost perfect scenario. One distinct advantage of the C-section was that my abdominal stitches hurt so much that I barely noticed how sore and tired my other body parts were from (a) the hours of labor that had preceded the surgery and (b) the new onslaught of an every other hour nursing routine. If the truth be known, I felt like I had been hit by a Mack truck and dragged for ten blocks before being jettisoned into the nearest brick building.

Our next door neighbor had called the day after the baby was born to express her delight at David-Andrew's arrival and during the conversation asked casually how the Caesarean would affect my being able to return to work as scheduled.

"Hardly at all, Dot," I blithely responded. "I'll have a little extra recovery time, that's all. You'll see me backing out of the driveway heading to the office in no time. I mean really, how hard can it be to manage one little bitty seven-pound baby?"

I thought I detected a slight chuckle as Dot, mother of five, grandmother of seven, hung up.

As I hung up the phone, I looked down at the blissfully sleeping infant in my arms and was convinced that this was going to be a piece of cake. Little did I know that, "How hard can it be to manage one little bitty seven pound baby?" was to become my mantra over the next few weeks.

We rounded the corner for home and pulled into the driveway. Alan parked the car in the garage, and we walked into the house. After laying David-Andrew in his new cradle, I looked at Alan for a moment. We smiled at one another.

Since Alan was a father twice over from his prior marriage, I asked, "Well, now what?"

"Well, there are really only three things you need to do: feed him, keep him warm and dry, and love him."

Sounded pretty simple to me. I could relate to this approach. It was a lot like the approach I took with most of my sales presentations - The Three Keys to Successful Investing, The Three Most Important Characteristics of a Mutual Fund, Three Simple Steps to Achieving Financial Independence.

I took great comfort at first from this simple three-step approach. Alan was supposed to know this stuff. He and his first wife already had two children. His credentials led me to believe that he was a pro. What I failed to gauge was his degree of uninvolvement with, his oblivion to, and his disinterest in the whole process the first time around. In truth Alan had been a "traditional" husband and father in his first marriage. In the parenting game he was as much of a rookie as I was. Wife number one had kept everything under control child-rearing-wise, so what was the big deal? Raising kids from his perspective was simple, simple, simple. As the next few days and months would prove, just because something is simple doesn't necessarily mean it's easy!

Having managed multi-million dollar budgets for several large enterprises and recruited and trained staffs of senior level executives, I had naturally assumed that I would certainly have adequate skills to keep one little bitty baby organized and in tow.

Not on your life!

Here I was - an educated, calm, cool, collected and experienced Wall Street executive well used to managing crisis situations - and at the drop of a hat I would find myself at wit's end, in an absolute tizzy because I could not seem to manage what appeared to be the simplest tasks for my new baby.

Sure, sure, I had heard about "post partum" blues but had never dreamed that I would succumb to the emotional depths that other wimpier females might have experienced. No, never, not me. None of those feminine emotional crying jags over which diaper rash cream to use or whether Pampers were superior to Luvs or whether (like the number of rings on my answering machine) to let the baby cry one second or three seconds or five seconds before picking him up. I had expected that I would rise above such common emotions usually associated with new mother anxiety with aplomb and handle each situation on a completely logical and wholly rational basis.

My basic error in reasoning was in assuming that because I could manage a business with ease, I could manage a baby equally well. Face it, there are a completely different set of skills involved with this baby business. I had avoided until now all contact and/or interest in the little creatures. In fact I had never been around babies and, unlike most teenage girls, had never even had one babysitting job in my life. So how was I to acquire the mothering skills that were needed for this new line of work?

Just because I was able to travel cross-country with ease meant nothing when I was trying to figure out how long I should let David-Andrew cry before picking him up. Sure I could navigate the streets of New York City like a native, but this definitely did not prepare me to become an adequate burper. This kid was not the least bit impressed that I could hold an audience of 500 in rapt attention during a seminar. At two o'clock in the morning when he had the sniffles, this was a totally irrelevant piece of trivia to David-Andrew.

I had plenty of common sense when it came to selling complicated leveraged private placement equipment leasing limited partnerships, but absolutely none when it came to something as seemingly simple as bathing a baby!!

Without fail, I would get out the little plastic tub, baby soap and shampoo, cotton balls, swabs and the baby brush. Then I'd carefully check the water temperature with my elbow as all the books recommended, plop in the baby and the rubber ducky toy, get him lathered up and then realize that I had forgotten his special monogrammed baby towel, or a dry diaper, or the baby powder.

Alan would find the baby happily splashing in the tub while I stood over him, my nails digging into my palms and tears streaming down my cheeks, totally frustrated with my utter incompetence. In retrospect, I know that my emotional ups and downs were being influenced by the rivers of hormones that were coursing through my body which was trying to get readjusted after giving birth. I always thought that if someone ever plotted the variation in my hormone levels the first month or two after David-Andrew was born, the resulting chart would have looked a lot like the daily graphs of the Standard and Poor's 500 during a particularly volatile stock market.

My little ovaries were totally confused and didn't know whether to stay on vacation or get back into the swing of things. Their supervisor was clearly not providing them with adequate direction either. They didn't know whether to produce estrogen or progesterone nor in what combination. I would have happily settled for a higher blood alcohol content until they made up their mind, but since I was nursing, indulging in my craving for a good glass of Cabernet Sauvignon was quickly ruled out as a wise course of action.

A second contributing factor to my emotional volatility index was sleep deprivation. And I thought that my obsession with getting enough sleep had disappeared after the fourth month of pregnancy. Little did I know that it would simply lie latent until triggered again following the arrival of the baby.

I actually had believed the statistics in all those baby books I devoured which stated that new born babies sleep 90 percent of the time. Obviously this is an average. Somewhere in the world there are babies who sleep 145 percent of the time because David-Andrew only slept 35 percent!

Boy, do I have vivid recollections of stumbling around our living room and dining room - David-Andrew in his Snuggli wailing with a tummy ache - for hours in the wee small hours of the morning. Whenever he would start to get quiet, I would think, "Good. Now I can sit down." I would approach the closest couch or chair, begin my descent, only to be propelled back to my marching position by indignant screams.

After pacing relentlessly from room to room nonstop for two or three hours, I would begin to wonder if it was possible for me to fall asleep while pacing back and forth. The mere thought of such a calamity would fill me with panic that I might indeed fall and injure David-Andrew in the process. This anxiety jolt was enough to produce sufficient adrenalin to keep me awake for a few more hours.

I still think there is no lonelier feeling than being up (awake would be too strong a word, it implies alertness) at 2:45 a.m. in a dead-still house and none more frustrating than sharing that experience with a baby who does not feel well.

Are you now asking yourself, "Where was her husband during all this?" A very good question. As all good husbands know, it is their job to get a good night's sleep so that at least one of the conjugal pair will remain alert and not have their intellectual processes impaired by the sleep deprivation thing. And Alan was a very good husband.

While this lack of sleep was unnerving, I felt much more fortunate than my childhood friend, Pam. She was a highly successful and well respected elementary school principal and mother of a baby boy, Ray, who literally did not sleep for fifteen months. This meant that she did not sleep either.

Each morning she would prepare herself for work, load the baby and all his essential paraphernalia in the car and drop him at her sitter's. She would proceed to school where she managed 1,500 youngsters and a teaching staff of fifty all day, pick up the baby at the sitter's, return home and experience the same sleepless routine every night. She finally came close to having a nervous breakdown as a result.

At the time Pam was coping with Ray's colic, I was less than empathetic. I strongly felt that she should have been able to do something - take Ray to the doctor, give him a pill, take charge somehow - to remedy this disruption to house and home. Coming from the school of opinion that children should be seen and not heard, I believed that for Ray to tyrannize his parents this way was unthinkable.

Back then I'd felt about Pam the way I felt about watching a mother whose child was throwing a temper tantrum in the middle of Bonwit Teller. "Just tell the kid to knock it off," I'd think. "There's just no excuse for that kind of behavior. You should DO something." My feeling was that any mother worth her salt simply would not allow her child to act that way. Boy, have I been humbled. Now that the mantle of motherhood has been flung around my shoulders, I find that my outlook has totally changed. That old Indian saying about not judging someone until you have walked a mile in her moccasins really came home to roost.

Finally, in desperation, Pam did do something - she hired a nun to move in every other weekend to take care of Ray so she and Paul, her long suffering husband could check into the Hilton and sleep for two days. Now age ten, Ray is a terrific little guy who has no idea how he tormented his poor mother.

David-Andrew never caused this level of sleeplessness for his mother I am happy to report. However, I did pull my share of all-nighters when he was tiny while keeping up a full business schedule as well. The challenge of "running on empty" from no sleep really became an issue when he was two and a half and I accepted a new position in Wisconsin as president of a mutual fund and broker/dealer organization, precipitating our relocation to a new house in a new city. Apparently experiencing some sort of separation anxiety triggered by this cross-country change, David-Andrew became afraid to go to sleep at night in his own room, so I found myself "camping out" on the stairway landing right outside his door to calm and reassure him until he'd fall asleep.

At first this did not cause a huge inconvenience for me. Once David-Andrew was tucked in, I almost looked forward to my hour or so perched on the top step where I would catch up on my business reading, review budgets, or work through the day's correspondence that my secretary had prepared for my signature. Since I was involved in the start up of a new company, my "homework" was considerable. I would probably have been up working on this anyway, I told myself, so I might as well be here. Now can you picture Al Neuharth getting his weekly column for *USA Today* written under these circumstances? Or Warren Buffet plotting corporate strategy while perched on a semi-dark stair landing? I also assumed that with the assurance that Mom was close at hand, David-Andrew would doze off quickly and that as soon as he felt comfortable with his new room and surroundings, he would revert to his usual angelic sleeping pattern in a few weeks.

Not so. Not only did this sentry duty go on for weeks, and then months, but even once I'd finally slip into bed David-Andrew began to wake up several times during the night. Sometimes after I'd been awakened multiple times, escorted him to the potty innumerable times and fetched uncountable glasses of water, my biorhythms were so out of whack I simply could not get back to sleep at all.

My colleagues at work were fascinated with my ability to be "conned" by this thirty pound manipulator since I can be tough as nails with employees who do not toe the line. So, who can be cross when wakened by a toddler standing at the side of your bed, nose to nose with you, blankie draped over his neck, pacifier in his mouth, glow worm tucked under one arm and Pat The Bunny under the other, singing "Ba Ba Black Sheep"?

I was getting less and less sleep, and the demands of my new job were physically and mentally exhausting enough without the added stress of no sleep. I began to welcome my trips out of town to make presentations to sales staff or to attend a financial conference for a whole new reason. I could kill two birds with one stone. While accomplishing my business purpose, I could also catch up on some long overdue sleep.

When it was at all possible, I would plan to arrive at my destination early the evening before the event would begin. If I were flying, this gave me an opportunity to nap on the plane. As soon as I would check into the hotel, find my room, and tip the bellhop, I'd throw my hanging bag in the closet and immediately head for the bed. I'd call the front desk telling them to hold all calls and then slip between the sheets with sincere mental apologies to my friend, Pam. Any shreds of guilt about not being able to comfort David-Andrew for a day or two drifted away as my head hit the pillow, where I would sleep uninterrupted for fourteen hours. It was bliss!

What I found curious about this situation in retrospect was that David-Andrew refused to sleep at night but had no trouble taking LONG naps when his nanny was with him during the day.

My mother provided me with no sympathy whatsoever during this period. "Oh, for heavens sake, Rochelle. Just let him cry himself to sleep for a few nights, and he'll be fine. It's just like acclimating a new puppy."

Right.

Easy for her to say. Not lugging around the corporate mother guilt (with a capital G) that I wagged around with me, and not having to listen to the pathetic whimpering or outright wailing coming from David-Andrew's room, and transmitting her helpful hints to me while sitting peacefully 1,500 miles away in Canada, she could afford to be objective!

In the years B.B. (Before Baby) Alan and I had belonged to that demographic group known as DINKs - Dual Income, No Kids - or as my friend Jane would say, "MINKs, dahling, MINKs. You know, Multiple Income, No Kids." I always assumed that the next step would be into the ranks of WOOFs - Well Off, Old Folks, not TICKs - Two Income Couple with Kids - or DISCs - Dual Income, Sleepless Couple. DISC didn't really fit though because only one of us was sleepless but you get the picture. I finally labeled myself a CHASM - Career-oriented, Harried And Sleepless Mother - and, boy, did that one fit!

As the weeks ticked on, I began to seriously worry about my standards. One of my mottos has always been, "Mediocrity sucks." Right about now I would have been delighted with mediocre. Being an average kind of mom sounded like something I could be happy with. Frankly I would have equated it with being nominated for the Nobel Peace Prize on some days.

Just getting dressed in the morning became as challenging as pitching a room full of investment bankers on the merits of buying Penn Central junk bonds. I had naively told anyone who might listen that once I had the baby, instead of starting the day with my standard 7:30 a.m. daily breakfast meeting, I would just schedule a 7:45 a.m. meeting. After all, I reasoned, that would give me another fifteen minutes in my morning routine to get the baby ready.

Fifteen minutes did not even begin to approach the additional time I found I needed to integrate one small human child into my morning routine. Since I was nursing, I was up at 5:30 a.m. for the morning feeding, during which time I would either doze, read yesterday's *Wall Street Journal* (I perpetually became a day behind on all the business news), or jot down my notes for the day's activities. After David-Andrew was fed, I'd shove his wriggling body into clean clothes, strap him into his infant seat, pop a pacifier in his mouth, wrap his little fist around a rattle and station him on the bathroom floor.

I would then undress and hop into the shower. Without fail, just as I would lather my hair with shampoo either the pacifier would slip from his lips, or I would hear the rattle clatter across the floor, and he would invariably begin to howl. Peering through the suds running down my face, usually with only one eye open to avoid a stinging sensation in both eyes, I would pop my head out of the shower door, smiling widely, with a cheery "Hi, baby. Here's Mommy."

At this point he would always stop crying, either in utter delight at the magical reappearance of his mother or in horror at the sight of a sopping wet head, dripping white sudsy foam with only one eye and a voice like his mother - I was never sure which. But as soon as the shower door would close, the crying would commence again.

While I found his despair heart wrenching, after an almost non-stop peek-a-boo routine consisting of more than a few dozen "Hi, baby. Here's Mommy"'s I was finding that just taking a shower in the morning was becoming a protracted task, totally blowing my time schedule to smithereens. And I still had to dry my hair, put on make up, and dress before dashing out to make my meeting.

In sharp contrast to my pre-baby days of going out the door fresh and well prepared, I was usually frazzled and exhausted - and the day was only starting. My hair, still damp and already starting to droop in spite of the massive amounts of anti gravity spray I had used, looked like it should have been on the head of someone gracing the cover of *Rolling Stones*. The aroma of my perfume was being overpowered by that of baby drool and Gerber's oatmeal which had been smeared on my neck when I picked up the baby for a last minute hug before leaving and which I merely swiped at with a tissue as I walked out the door to get into the car.

The results of my efforts to entertain David-Andrew while simultaneously "doing my face" were often disastrous. I've seen better make up jobs on eight year-olds. Running out of time at home, I would throw my makeup bag in my purse and try to put on the rest in the car. I attempted to apply my mascara at stop lights resulting in a look that would be more becoming to a raccoon or a character in the Addams family. Spitting on an already soggy tissue to repair smeared makeup may not be the accepted practice that high falutin models recommend, but it became a standard part of my morning ritual.

And my mind, oh my God, my mind. Instead of feeling like a steel trap, it was more like a sieve. I could just feel those facts and ideas seeping away as I parked the car and headed for the restaurant to meet my client or colleague. It was a grueling experience.

About this time I had read an article in a popular magazine designed for new mothers called "Simplify Your Life and Ease Your Pressures." No problem. My life was simple - simply overwhelming.

As I have reflected back on those horrors of the first few weeks as a new mother, it has occurred to me that clearly executive motherhood is an occupation that could use the serious attention of a top notch training consultant. Face it. While Mother Nature programs mother birds, raccoons and such with natural instincts to deal with their new roles, where are the training manuals, where are the "how to" video and audio tapes, where are the workshops and seminars that can help us develop the maternal skills we need to cope with the integration of baby and career we so desperately want? Sure Dr. Spock and a few others have produced a paperback or two, but nothing in depth from someone who can appreciate this situation we are in.

Fred Pryor, are you listening?

I'm serious about this.

Actually when David-Andrew was about nine-months-old and I was finally getting the hang of my new duties as a mom, I became convinced that there really was a market for an "Executive Woman's Guide To Motherhood" video. Ever one with an entrepreneurial soul, I lined up a video professional, wrote what I deemed a terrific script, and "borrowed" a brand new baby from a neighbor down the street (not a member of the Screen Actors Guild but he received a $500 savings bond for his efforts).

The video company brought in ten tons of lights and equipment and more personnel than Cecil B. DeMille used for *The Ten Commandments*. After filming for more than twelve hours we called it a wrap. One week later ABC announced that Joan Lunden had produced exactly the same thing! So, with my checkbook considerably lighter by the down payment on my latest "brainstorm", I had been foiled again.

CHAPTER 9. THE GALLOPING GOURMET

La Leche never told me it would be like this.

Several years ago, before David-Andrew was even a gleam in Alan's and my eyes, I was rushing through the Atlanta airport when the front of a magazine in the window of the gift shop caught my eye. On the cover was a Yuppie Mom, dressed in a grey skirted suit, white all-cotton blouse, and silk floppy bow tie. In one hand she carried a brown leather brief case and *The Wall Street Journal*, in the other she held an infant pretty enough to appear on a jar of Gerber's. Knee high were two little tykes all decked out in Calvin Klein for kids, one on each side, clutching her skirt. All three children were howling, tears streaming down their faces, and frankly the Mom looked like she would "lose it" at any moment.

I've forgotten the exact caption splashed under the picture, something about "Working Mothers: The New Breed."

I can remember stopping, looking at the magazine cover for two or three seconds, and then resuming my assault on the concourse, thinking "Thank heavens I don't have THAT to contend with." Really, a room full of middle-aged stockbrokers was enough to handle and still keep my professional grace in tact. How was I to know then that I would live to eat those words and become one of the new breed myself?

I had a secretary once who was a working mom with five kids. I'll admit that I wasn't totally sensitive to some of her requests to leave early to attend a child's school play or basketball game, nor was I sympathetic when she called in to take a sick day because her baby had the chicken pox. After all, what about me? We had a business to run, phones to answer, letters to write, investments to sell.

She had a coffee cup on her desk that I'll never forget. On the front of the cup was a picture of a working mom that looked suspiciously like the magazine cover in the Atlanta airport, same Yuppie Mom, briefcase, distraught kids, dogged expression and all. The difference is that I do remember the caption that appeared under the illustration and in twenty words succinctly summed up the whole situation, "I am a working mother. I have a job. I keep a house. I have a family. I am nuts."

I found out later that her husband had given her the cup for Mother's Day. I guess it was better than getting a power drill, but I considered it a pretty unromantic gift myself. What about champagne, flowers, diamond earrings, a vasectomy?

These two mental images popped into my head as I again found myself back in the Atlanta airport on my way to a national sales meeting six weeks after David-Andrew's birth, the "I am nuts" part seeming especially appropriate.

Getting back into the swing of executive travel wasn't all that tough for me. I was able to get down the airplane aisles with relative ease now, and my feet obediently slipped back into my shoes at the end of each flight. There was just one little bitty complication.

When at the age of thirty-seven , I learned that I was pregnant and was going to have it all, I also decided to DO it all, too. And that included breast feeding. I had read of the dangers of instigating formula feeding too early (allergies, don't you know? - and my family is plagued with them). So, two and a half weeks following David-Andrew's arrival I sneaked back into the office and decided that I could nurse the baby when I was home and express extra milk for nanny Kathy to use while I was gone.

The child care books made it sound like a breeze - really simple. Perhaps for someone raised on a Minnesota dairy farm who is well acquainted with the theory behind Surge Milking Machines, but apparently not for someone from a Canadian fishing camp. I tried every brand of hand held mechanical breast pump on the market, throwing $200 or so at the effort in the process, buying every contraption advertised, and frankly I was a miserable failure only able to eke out meager amounts of liquid refreshment for the precious babe. If this had been a work related issue, I would have hired a consultant; but, face it, this is not exactly the sort of project for which consultants are readily available. Where would you find one? Under milking machines in the yellow pages?

AGAIN, I reached for the phone to call my friend Jane in Boston, who in her most proper Boston accent and without the slightest hint of sympathy in her voice proclaimed, "Oh, Rochelle, get into the twentieth century. Buy an electric breast pump!"

"Alan, quick, come here," I shouted as I hung up the phone.

"Now what?"

"Jane says we need to get an electric breast pump. She says the mechanical ones are beastly and the electrics are a breeze. Will you buzz out and see what you can find?"

"Are you serious? Where do I find one of these contraptions? K-Mart? Walgreen's? Army Surplus?"

"Oh, don't be difficult, Alan, we're on to something here. Just run down to a medical supply store. They'll have lots of them."

After he discovered that the first store he visited wanted $750 to buy an electric breast pump, Alan visited every medical supply house in Denver looking for something a little more reasonable. He figured that the first store must have been featuring the Dolly Parton version and told them we could use something a little more modest.

"Best one on the market," he was told.

"Could be," Alan replied, "but we would settle for something a little thriftier."

As it turned out, thrifty meant rental. Well, why not? I'd only need it for five or six months. Then the pediatrician and I had agreed David-Andrew could be introduced to formula.

So later that afternoon, as I sat in the kitchen with the baby in my lap, reading the mail, I heard Alan come in the front door.

"Where do you want me to put this thing?" he asked.

"What's wrong with the kitchen counter?" was my response.

"Are you kidding? There won't be any room."

What was he talking about?

Panting and puffing from exertion, Alan proudly carried the pump into the kitchen.

"So where do you want this?"

I looked up. Oh my God, the thing was the size of the generator my brother-in-law has on the back of his motor home.

"Alan, there must be some mistake. That must be the dairy size. We just need a baby size pump."

"This IS the baby size pump. So where do you want it?"

"Good Lord, not here in the kitchen. How about the sun room?"

And so the pump was ceremoniously installed in the sun room that I had so lovingly decorated to look like the solarium of an English country manor house that I had seen in *Architectural Digest*. It was filled with wicker furniture covered in a gorgeous fabric (black with multi-colored pansies) and overflowing with plant life.   And here in its midst was a piece of gleaming chrome high technology fitted with dials and gauges reminiscent of the cockpit of the T3 Piper Cub aircraft I flew at Dad's fishing camp. I felt right at home the first time I used it, instrument rated and all. The editors of *Architectural Digest* would have had apoplexy!

During my maiden flight when I first hooked up the pump and flipped all the appropriate knobs and switches, I noticed an interesting sensation. It was very,

very soothing. No wonder cows are always so contented. As long as Elsie was hooked up to a milking machine twice a day she could really mellow out!

As it turned out the electric milk pump was a real time saver. Instead of spending forty minutes manhandling myself with various combinations of tubes and funnels that are supposed to express milk, now I could hook up and have my hands free to hold *The Wall Street Journal* or *Business Week*. Boy, did I feel like the efficient executive now. And before taking a business trip I would "milk" myself more often to save up enough for Kathy to use while I was gone. Thank you, dear Jane.

So what's the little bitty complication already, you're asking yourself about now. Get to the point. Well, the point is that it's a little tough to lug a full size electric breast pump the size of a diesel engine onto the Eastern Shuttle. So traveling did become a bit complex. Using the breast pump before going on a trip was great for the baby, but what about the Mom? When I was away, David-Andrew still ate those great gourmet meals. But since there was no baby to nurse, I would become engorged.

Big deal, you're thinking. Take one of those mechanical pumps with you. You've got dozens. Exactly. And I did. Except for the first trip that I took to New York thirty days after the baby was born. I'll admit it; I was a little unorganized. I did a great job of getting things ready for Alan, David-Andrew, and nanny Kathy. I did slightly less well for myself.

Running behind schedule, I gunned my car for the airport. As I was mentally picturing the items I had in my suitcase, I gasped when I realized that the manual breast pump did NOT get packed. I could still see it on the bathroom counter next to my sink. This constituted a real emergency.

I pulled off the freeway and wheeled into the parking lot of the nearest baby supply store, and slammed on the brakes with a screech. Hurtling myself through the front door I shouted, "Breast pump!" The manager, a young man just out of school with a degree in retailing, came to my assistance. He rushed me over to a counter and began explaining the features and benefits of a brand new, revolutionary portable electric breast pump from Gerber. And for only $49.95! Wait 'til I tell Alan about THIS, I mentally gloated.

Well, at $49.95 I decided it was obviously better than a manual one, paid the bright young fellow and raced to the airport. As I sat on the plane, I kept thinking about how smart I had been and that this little portable model would really make travel much simpler. Maybe I could nurse David-Andrew for more than six months. These thoughts, though pleasant, were definitely premature.

My body did not know of course that there was no baby traveling with me and so continued to produce nourishing milk during the three and a half hour flight from Denver to New York City, as well as the hour it took to get from the airport to my hotel in Midtown. I checked into the Grand Hyatt as quickly as possible and beat a hasty retreat to my room where I ripped off my clothes, plugged in the pump and prepared to disengorge my swollen and painful mammary glands.

As I flipped on the pump switch, I was horrified to hear a dull humming rather than the perky pumping sound that should have been emitting from this product. Gerber may have been great when it came to strained prunes, but they didn't know beans about electronics. The solenoid in the switch was defective, and I was miles away from a replacement.

Grimacing with every gesture, I found it necessary to manually express the milk in the bathroom and wish longingly for my pump almost 2,000 miles away in Denver. And who was I going to tell this to? Who of my colleagues could relate to this? What did Jay Chazanoff know about nursing mothers? What did the portfolio managers care?

OK, fine, but just wait til I land in Denver, I fumed mentally. That baby supply store will be my first stop on the way home and, boy, is that kid going to get a real piece of my mind.

In the middle of the night I had a brainstorm. Thinking I had found a brilliant solution to my problem, the next morning at the crack of dawn I called three of the closest New York hospitals to see if they would like any milk donations. (Hospitals frequently advertise for mother's milk.) Each hospital was very sweet on the phone, but because I was from out of town, they weren't interested. I'm still not sure why imported milk was unacceptable, but there you have it.

So for two days while maintaining my busy schedule of meetings, phone calls and conferences, I manually expressed my milk and was bruised from my waist to my neck by the time I climbed back on the plane headed for Denver. I imagined the flight attendants looking at my neck bruises and then each other. I knew they were convinced that I was the victim of some jealous husband or lover who had tried unsuccessfully to choke me to death, and here I was bravely carrying on with my life. That was certainly a more colorful explanation than telling them I was actually the victim of a malfunctioning solenoid in my breast pump.

After takeoff, I headed for the lavatory where I glumly expressed milk into the little metal lavatory sink. The sound reminded me of Old MacDonald's farm where Molly the milkmaid tended to Bossy the cow. I swear I can still hear that metallic ringing sometimes, when I'm alone in the lav of a 767 at 40,000 feet and the wind is just right.

When I wasn't traveling, the whole nursing routine became the ultimate exercise in logistics. My being in the right place at the right time severely taxed my secretary to the max as she would squeeze meetings, conferences, and phone calls around the dietary whims of a three week old baby. New babies have very small tummies. This means that instead of eating a lot several times a day, they eat little bitty amounts - but often - like every few hours.

My usual procedure was to nurse David-Andrew before leaving for the office in the morning, leaving enough pumped milk for the mid-morning snack. I would dash out of the office at lunch time to feed the baby again and this time leave more pumped milk for the mid-afternoon snack. Finally at 5:30 p.m., I would jump in my car, deftly maneuvering through the rush hour traffic - all the time hoping and praying that the baby was not screaming at the top of his lungs with hunger - pull into the garage, start to unbutton my blouse as the automatic garage door was closing and I was getting out of the car so as not to slow down dinner for the wee master, rush into the house and collapse into a chair with the baby at my breast. Thus did I vacillate between business executive and wet nurse for months.

It occurred to me during one of my mad dashes to become the feed bag that any male captain of industry would have found such an intrusion on his business life totally unacceptable, not to mention bizarre. I mean, can't you just picture the late Malcolm Forbes hopping on his Harley Davidson and gunning his motorcycle on the freeway just so he wouldn't miss feeding time for Junior?

At this point, my life was beginning to feel a little out of control. I was starting to wonder if I might have underestimated slightly how easy it would be to work this small bundle of joy into my life. The first time nanny Kathy called asking where the bottle of expressed milk was because it was feeding time and she couldn't find it anywhere, I sheepishly had to admit that in the morning rush I must have experienced a severe case of brain fade because I had forgotten to leave any.

The baby was bellowing in the background at about the decibel level of a jet airliner ready for take off, so I knew this definitely classified as an emergency. Trying to look calm and collected, I left the office after telling Teresa that I had to run to an emergency meeting (true) and would be back momentarily (not true since it took me twenty-five minutes to drive home, another twenty-five to nurse, and twenty-five more minutes for the return trip to the office).

As the baby grew, so did his hunger. This imposed some additional complications on a schedule that was already starting to look like a flow chart for assembling the MX missile. Now that his little tummy could handle more ounces of milk, he wanted MORE. Nanny Kathy would call and tell me that David-Andrew had inhaled all the milk I had left, and he was still hungry.

If my schedule would not permit me to leave the office, many's the time she would bundle up the baby and bring him to me. Kathy would hand me the baby and then park herself outside my closed office door with a good book. On the other side of the door I would sit at my desk, blouse unbuttoned, with a nursing babe in my lap while I called my staff in New York, read the day's mail, or proofed the blue lines for our latest marketing sales brochure.

While nursing is a wonderful way to bond with a newborn and, I'm convinced, improves the child's immunization faculties as well as guards against allergies, frankly I was beginning to feel like the mascot for Land O'Lakes dairy co-op. Honestly, I was either nursing or pumping.

I did feel more fortunate than our marketing assistant, Peggy, who had a baby a year earlier and had also chosen to nurse. She was unable to get away during the day to nurse so she kept expressed milk at home for the sitter to use. The problem was not with the baby. The baby got plenty to eat. The problem was that for the eight hours that Peggy was in the office her breasts were becoming the size of watermelons, and about that hard.

Peggy was from Little Rock and decidedly a little rough around the edges. "It's just not too cool," she would drawl, "when you start leaking milk like a faucet during a client presentation."

Not too cool at all.

Peggy took all her coffee breaks and lunch hours in the ladies room. No, she was not powdering her nose or checking her mascara as the entire male population of the office concluded. She was sitting on the john with her dress open to her waist, nursing bra unhooked, breast pump activated, expressing milk into a little glass bottle which she would take home for junior's lunch tomorrow.

When she was done, she would clean the pump, put it in one brown paper bag and put the bottle of milk into a second brown paper bag which she then put in the refrigerator until time to go home.

Peggy's ultimate humiliation occurred one day when Wayne, our resident computer techno-nerd, was rummaging through the office fridge, pulled out Peggy's brown bag and looked inside.

"Hey, everybody," he queried as he waved the bottle of pale bluish liquid around, "what the hell is THIS?"

To quote Peggy, "I liked to die!"

For sure.

CHAPTER 10. THE NANNY TRAP

Rent-A-Wife meets Super Mom.

As I have thought about the successful implementation of having it all (between plane trips, board meetings and glasses of spilled milk), I've identified that the answer to the question, "How the heck am I going to do this?" has been to surround myself with a highly capable staff of support folks.

My original game plan called for hiring a full-time nanny because I did know, even during those early days of supreme naiveté, that having a top-notch care giver would be essential to even coming close to pulling off this having it all business.

I knew that choosing the right person to fill a job description that read like an apprentice for the Virgin Mary was going to be a critical decision. After making the rounds of the handful of Denver personnel agencies specializing in "domestics" and doling out my $500 registration fee (which would be applied against their fee of ten percent of the first years wages), I settled on an agency called "Rent-A-Mom" to do the initial screening for me. (This was after being completely intimidated by one very posh agency whose chic director, garbed in enough Ralph Lauren to have sent Ralph and his entire family to Hawaii for a month, informed me that their personnel were "very special." Obviously an agency catering to snobs, all the parents were carefully screened, given a battery of tests and forced to relate name, rank, serial number, social register placement, annual salary and net worth. I sensed Alan and I just were not special enough.)

Working with Rent-A-Mom, I reasoned, would make hiring the ideal person a less time consuming process. As it turned out, even with Rent-A-Mom's help, meeting with potential candidates was more like a full time job.

The interviewing process was fascinating. First, I got LOTS of applicants. It was amazing to see how many folks wanted to take care of other people's offspring. If you have seen *Baby Boom* and thought that Diane Keaton's interviewees were all invented by some extravagantly imaginative studio writer with a couple of screws loose, I can assure you these movie roles didn't come close to the cast of characters I encountered.

I had one wizened old grandmother not a day under seventy, false teeth clattering as she talked, who had little bottles of vodka from the airlines in her purse; a high school dropout with a halter top, Sony Walkman, and tattoo of a Coor's beer can on her forearm; a middle aged applicant who had recently graduated from the Denver Police Academy and reminded me of the stereotypical Swedish masseuse (and with about the same sense of humor); several former fast food specialists; and one beady eyed, narrow lipped, prim and proper spinster type instructor of a British nanny academy whose description of her child rearing philosophy seemed to be a recitation of the management principles of Attila the Hun and General Patton.

This last one conveyed to me, in all confidence of course, that she had been highly desired as the number one choice of Prince Charles and Princess Diana, but she found the living accommodations somewhat below her standards. (Buckingham Palace below her standards?) I began to despair that we would ever find the right person to nurture Baby Wallach.

Understand that I was not new to this nanny thing. I had been raised by a nanny, Belle McCubbah. Belle, who hailed from Scotland, had been responsible for raising me until she suffered a heart attack. My four sisters and I were then governed by three successive nanny/housekeepers over the next thirty years while my mother worked with Dad to build up our fishing lodge business. Since we had all, seemingly at least, turned out to be bright and reasonably well adjusted kids I was comfortable with the nanny concept.

Throughout the whole nanny search process, though, I have to admit I was fairly frequently plagued with doubts. I worried about whether this person would fit into our family, would she be kind to Baby, could I trust her, would I be able to pay her enough, would I pay her too much, what personal qualities were the most important, would she be an adequate surrogate mother, and that killer question - should I really go back to work at all? Could I?

This from me, a woman who was totally committed to her career, who had decided from the outset that Baby would not interfere with my becoming a company president before I was forty. What must other women deal with, I agonized, other women who don't have the resources or options that I do? It was a real revelation to me that these would be issues that would concern me - EVER. And so I continued to interview as I fervently prayed, "Please, God, you know I need help. Send me Super Nanny." And She did.

With Belle in mind, my original image of the perfect nanny candidate was a generously bosomed, motherly, grey haired lady with an appealing lilting brogue who was a veteran of the Mary Poppins school of child rearing. What I got was anything but that.

Kathy Schmidt was a very attractive Minnesota farm girl, young (definitely NOT thirty-something or even close), vivacious, clean cut and good humored. By education, Kathy was a licensed practical nurse whose first job was in the neonatal department of Mayo Clinic's St. Mary's Hospital. Since I would not have recognized an ear infection from colic or the measles from diaper rash, Kathy's medical background was highly attractive to me. She articulated the wholesome, Midwestern values that she learned in her small town, large family background - the same values that seem to have spawned an entire industry that recruits nannies for wealthy New York City and Boston professional families.

Remember *The Sound of Music*? Remember Julie Andrews playing the role of the nanny who left the cloister to work for Colonel Von Trapp? She frolicked through the meadows of Austria with his brood after cutting up old curtains from the children's bedroom to make play clothes for them and when it stormed she gathered all the children into bed with her, so they would not be frightened by the thunder. Well, in contrast to the weird characters I had interviewed so far, Kathy came very close to the governess standards presented in this film classic.

Not only did Kathy have medical qualifications, she had experience! She had been a nanny for over two years for one of the wealthiest families in Denver. Her previous employer had a 12,000 square foot house. It was so large that as part of the security system, they had installed an electronic mapping network to identify where people were walking in the house. Their friends were definitely high calibre. Ted Kennedy had come to visit! They had two chefs, a chauffeur, two maids and a back up nanny. Kathy lived in and had her own private apartment. We certainly were not in this league. Kathy was going to be chief cook and bottle washer at the Wallach house.

Kathy was exactly what I wanted and needed and I made up my mind to hire her in the first ten minutes of our interview. Kathy firmly declared that she had no intention of living in. When we talked about salary, she announced that she was "expensive - but worth it." Since I've always felt that you get what you pay for I was willing to pay up for a pro. By the time Kathy left us over four and a half years later, she had relocated with us from Colorado to Wisconsin and had enjoyed raises that boosted her salary to just shy of $19,000 a year, joined us on two or three trips each year (usually to a nice resort in connection with business), drove a "company car" - the only new car in the household, enjoyed three weeks annual vacation and was worth every single penny!

Kathy had aspirations of going back to college to get her degree and she definitely had a predisposition for the caring, nurturing, social service arts, but was short on financial resources to support herself as a full time student. She came into our lives with her capable take charge style and literally saved the day, making it possible for me to juggle my professional and domestic roles with some semblance of sanity.

Under nanny Kathy's capable tutelage, within a few weeks of delivery I began to master part of my mothering job description, or else I was just so numb from lack of sleep that I ceased to be so hard on myself about my lack of skill. By the time David-Andrew was eight weeks old, I was getting a little bit cocky and beginning to feel like an old hand at this executive/mother role. That was before I was without a nanny for a week. For five crazed days, I had my chance to live through the frantic morning ritual that the majority of working mothers in America experience each and every day. Talk about instant humility!

Nanny Kathy had told me months earlier during our initial interview that she would need to be out of town for a week in late May for her parent's fortieth wedding anniversary. Certainly this was an important family function, and I had agreed that she should attend. (This was during my how-hard-can-it-be-to-manage-a-six-pound-baby, what-me-worry phase of pregnancy.)

Now the time was upon us. After grilling every mother I knew about the finest day care provider in the city, I had finally been able to make temporary arrangements for the week with the top pick, Mrs. Musil.

So how tough can this be? I asked myself. Kathy will only be gone for a week. I can endure ANYTHING for a week. I'll just get up a little bit earlier to allow for the additional fifteen minute drive time to the baby sitter's. Other than that, it should be **almost** like having nanny Kathy here.

Sunday night I set the alarm for 5:00 a.m., a full half-hour before usual, feeling that this was really being very generous and sheepishly thinking that I was probably a little paranoid about how much extra time it would take me to get organized and make the drive to the sitter on Monday morning.

HAH! If they ever give out awards for naiveté, I will definitely be a contender. What was I thinking?

I forgot that not only did I have to get myself ready as usual, get the baby changed and dressed, and nurse the baby, I also had to pack his diaper bag with extra clothes, diapers, toys and bottles. This had to be deposited in the car along with the baby car seat and the Port-A-Crib and Moses basket. The proper blankets had to be included as well, or little one would not sleep a peep all day. After half a dozen trips from house to car, I was finally ready to roll and I was already forty-five minutes behind schedule.

This isn't too bad, I told myself, as the baby and I whizzed down the freeway toward Mrs. Musil's place. Actually it was kind of nice to have this extra time to enjoy David-Andrew who was gurgling contentedly on the seat behind me.

When I came to a dead halt in traffic at the freeway entry ramp, I did begin to have a few reservations about this temporary child care arrangement. How was Mrs. Musil going to be able to watch seven other children and have any time to devote to my precious? What if David-Andrew cried all day? What if Mrs. Musil was a well intentioned but casual housekeeper? We had kept David-Andrew's environment as sterile as possible. What if the other children hurt the baby? What if . . . .

The mental images continued to race across my mind.

Halfway to Mrs. Musil's in the midst of my revery, I remembered that I had not included the vitamins in the diaper bag. Heaven forbid that the babe go for even one day without his Vitte Drops. He might develop rickets or pellagra or some other vitamin deficiency syndrome. Pulling over into the right hand lane of the freeway, I exited at the next opportunity, turned around, and headed back to the house.

I finally arrived at Mrs. Musil's an hour and a half later than originally planned where I reversed the car packing procedure and lugged everything into her house like a pack mule. I was the last mother to arrive, and she was already surrounded by five little toddlers. There was one baby in an infant seat and another older baby in a play pen. Mrs. Musil wore a serene expression; her house was impeccably clean and the youngsters seemed content.

"Now, don't worry about a thing, Mrs. Wallach," Mrs. Musil said. "David-Andrew will fit right in. I've already told the children we will have a visitor this week, and they're just delighted. They can't wait to meet him."

By that time I wasn't worried about the baby at all. I was wondering how early I was going to need to get up tomorrow morning in order to get to the office at a decent time.

Having a full-time, experienced professional nanny is, I recognize, a huge luxury and is one that I fully appreciate. As I drove to my office thanking my lucky stars that I had found, and could afford, someone as qualified as nanny Kathy, I cogitated on the notion that most working women are not nearly as fortunate. Their only choice budget-wise is to find a Mrs. Musil - and pray that she is as qualified as Mrs. Musil.

Mothers everywhere go through this routine EVERY morning - and sometimes with two or three tots in tow. By the time many of them get to work they've already been up and "working" for three to four hours. Lovely as Mrs. Musil was, it was not the same as having child care take place in your own home.

And what about the evening routine? Morning was a panic, but the evening pickup was pandemonium. I had to be sure to leave the office in plenty of time to be at Mrs. Musil's by 6:00 p.m. Not that I blamed her. If I had a house full of kids all day, I'd want some time to collect my wits, get out the bulldozer to pick up my house before tomorrow's onslaught, and spend some time with my own family. It's just that MY work day is rarely over by six. Well, for this week it would have to be.

Although I was the last mom to leave a child in the morning, I was the first to arrive for the evening pick up. As I pulled into Mrs. Musil's driveway, I was greeted by the sight of five little two- and three-year-old faces, noses pushed to the glass, pathetically looking for their own moms to come. My heart felt like it was being squeezed in a vise. My image at work was that of a tough cookie, but believe me, I was quickly becoming a marshmallow.

Kathy was a vital link in the total support system that bolstered my ability to have it all. To run a multi-million dollar business and keep my house from resembling one of the sets used on the TV program "Sanford & Son", I quickly came to the conclusion that I MUST give up guilt along with any Superwoman fantasies I might have been harboring. I gave up guilt in 1985, at which point I decided that if I couldn't hire out what needed to be done around the house, then it just wouldn't get done.

As a result I had assembled a competent support staff to do just that. In addition to Kathy as full-time nanny, the staff included: a garden service - every week six Vietnamese gentlemen under the careful direction of Mr. Wakamoto piled out of a pick up truck and descended upon our lawn with much equipment and good humor and an hour later left us with manicured grass and flower beds; my long-time housekeeper - Alice, who was supervised by Kathy, came three times a week armed with mop, broom, feather duster, and industrial strength chemicals to handle all the cleaning chores; and Poop Van Scoop - who advertised their services as the Tootsie Roll Patrol (their invoices proudly proclaimed that they were number one in the number two business and that they specialized in "close encounters of the turd kind") to pick up after our two poodles.

Not living in Los Angeles, I have never been able to take advantage of the services of Bundle of Convenience, a mobile baby service and supply company. They advertise that they deliver everything but the baby! Believe me if I lived in California, I would have been one of their charter customers.

Cooking and entertaining on the weekends are my idea of fun, so these domestic duties I continue to enjoy. However, anything else related to homemaking and housekeeping is done by a service provider.

I am extremely fortunate to have so much good help. To some people I probably appear to be rather self-indulgent and spoiled to boot. They may be right, but it has occurred to me that in the process of having it all that I have created my own little economy. I work fourteen-hour days so that four or five other folks can make a living.

While nanny Kathy's duties were primarily baby oriented, her job description was a broad one. In fact she acted as the Wallach House (not to be confused with Animal House) manager. Every month money was automatically transferred from my checking account into her household account out of which she wrote checks for groceries, dry cleaning, housekeeping services, etc. She did all the grocery shopping and ran all the errands - dry cleaning, post office, appliance repair shop - that otherwise would have eaten up my entire weekend leaving me no time for mothering, wife-ing, or just plain enjoying myself.

Kathy also did all the menu planning and cooked all our meals during the week. We enthusiastically ate whatever she cooked. While not a graduate of the Cordon Bleu, she was a very good cook. In close to five years, she only created one inedible disaster. All the holiday touches and decorating - Valentine's Day, Easter, Fourth of July, Halloween, Thanksgiving, Christmas - were the result of Kathy's efforts. The only way there were going to be any eggs in the Easter baskets or Jack-O-Lanterns for Halloween was if Kathy got it done - and she did, with style.

In Alan's and my view, Kathy was never a baby sitter. She was clearly a professional and working for us was her job. She always lived in her own apartment, showed up at our front door at 7:30 each morning and was there when I walked in between 6:30 and 7:00 every night, Monday through Friday. From the time I left until returning, she was in charge of David-Andrew's health, well being, and development. She took him to his doctor appointments, swimming class, museums, music lessons, and luncheon dates with his mom.

Once she walked out the door at the end of the day, if we needed child care, we were on our own. So I was like any other mother if Alan and I wanted to go to the movies on Saturday night trying to round up a gum-chewing, Pepsi-drinking, pizza-breathed baby sitter.

Because Kathy was so very crucial to our lives, we were more than just a little sensitive to her satisfaction with this arrangement and tried to provide as many perks as possible. She accompanied us on family and business trips to nice resorts in Hawaii, California and Florida, where she was nanny by day but on vacation at night. And every summer she spent a month in Canada with us. If she even began to look unhappy, we would arrange for a nice trip or give her a raise or reward her with something special. The "something specials" included a color TV, VCR, stereo with compact disc player, cross-country skis and all the clothing and gear that go with it. Bribes? Absolutely!! She was wonderful, and we were not above buying her loyalty.

Kathy even drove the only new car in the Wallach garage. After moving to Wisconsin, we realized that we needed to buy a new car, something with front wheel drive and road gripping tires to cope with the quantities of snow which covered the earth and streets 80 percent of the year. After much shopping and haggling with car dealers, we purchased a brand new 1988 Saab, having been lured by all the advertisements and the salesman's statements about how safe and reliable it was.

The original idea was that Alan would drive the Saab, and we would keep Alan's old car, a well-worn Volvo, for Kathy to drive during the day to tote the baby around in. However, once the Saab was parked in the driveway, we reconsidered this decision.

Looking at me intently Alan announced, "The Volvo has old tires, old brakes, old transmission. What if it breaks down when Kathy is taking the baby to the doctor? What if its brakes fail and she has a wreck? I really think that Kathy should drive the new car, so we won't have to worry about David-Andrew's safety."

Now up until then Junior had been transported in the Volvo with no difficulty or second thoughts on our part, but the more I thought about it, I realized that he

131

was right. Well, we certainly could NOT have our precious David-Andrew being transported in any marginally safe vehicle. Ralph Nader might have us arrested! So, of course, Kathy drove the brand new car with the leather seats and compact disc player, and Alan and I continued to drive the clunkers with the bald tires, dented fenders, and temperamental starter motors. Well, I am exaggerating JUST a little, but you get the idea of where our priorities were!!

Kathy worked for us for almost five years, endured a cross-country relocation (from Colorado to Wisconsin - I have to admit that we did bribe her with a $1,000 moving bonus), several in-town moves until we were more settled in our "permanent" home, countless road trips and all manner of crises, both great and small. She has now been able to go back to school for that nursing degree she wants so badly. We miss her on a day-to-day basis but still manage to see her often socially. She made an indelible impression on our son and a palpable difference in our lives. We probably never told her often enough how much we appreciated all she did because we assumed, like many of us do about satisfying relationships, that she would always be there.

Even though I had known that Kathy's plan from the start was to acquire her nursing degree - and doing that would mean ultimately leaving us - nevertheless I was not prepared when she finally made her announcement to me that she was leaving. She had been accepted at the university and would be starting classes in the fall.

"You what . . . you when?" I stammered.

This can't be happening to me was what I was thinking. How would I ever find anyone as good as Kathy? She was part of the family. She had been there from the first. I may have been her employer, but she had taught me about being a mom. How was I going to cope? In fact, not very well at first.

I experienced every one of Kubler-Ross' stages of grief, and after spending three weeks denying that Kathy was leaving (I was convinced this was only temporary insanity on her part and that she would come to her senses any day now), and two weeks being angry that she was (I'll admit it, I got a little huffy. Well, really, my feelings were hurt), I had about ten days to find a new nanny. Talk about panic!

Pulling out the now yellowed and dog-eared folder containing the nanny job description, I perused it again. There wasn't a thing on the list I would change. I was still looking for a Julie-Andrews -style-Mary-Poppins-type nanny. However, it seemed to me that someone older, cut out of my nanny Belle McCubbah's mold, might be more stable. This type of candidate probably would not have aspirations to go back to school and become a brain surgeon. Also, reasoning that Kathy may have experienced burn-out from the pace of our lives, I would cut back on some of my expectations and let this person relax just a teensy little bit.

Due to the brief ten-day hiring schedule I had left for myself, I was perhaps not quite as thorough with my interviews as before. Also, I was desperate. Kathy was leaving in two weeks. Alan and I couldn't take David-Andrew to work with us. We needed help, and quickly!

Enter one of our interim child care solutions, Betty, an older experienced housekeeper-type whose idea of child care was to plop David-Andrew in front of the TV while she went to put a load of wash in the machine. He spent so much time in front of television that he memorized all the commercials. When I came home at night he would follow me around the house reciting all the thirty second spots and catchy jingles word for word. One of his favorites was for Epilady, "no wax, no shaving" - this from the mouth of a four-year-old.

Kathy had been very careful about David-Andrew's nutrition - no junk food, no additives, no preservatives. Betty, on the other hand, was liberal to say the least.

Her idea of a balanced diet was Sugar Pops for breakfast, jelly sandwiches and Chips Ahoy for lunch, Ding Dongs, Ruffles, and root beer in between. The kid was on a perpetual sugar high.

Betty was certainly a kind individual, but without imagination. We tried to encourage Betty to play with David-Andrew. This was met with blank stares. We suggested perhaps she and David-Andrew could bake cookies together.

"Wouldn't that be messy?" was her response.

What about a walk around the block?

"My knees are shot, you know."

Could she ask some of David-Andrew's friends over to play in the yard?

"He'll get dirty."

One of the reasons we wanted a nanny was so David-Andrew could be involved in a blend of cultural and educational activities. We wanted someone who could help stimulate his mental development. Admittedly Betty had not held herself out as a rocket scientist, but I began to suspect that her idea of an intellectual activity was watching re-runs of "The Andy Griffith Show." At least David-Andrew preferred to watch "Sesame Street", the weather channel and "Wheel of Fortune." Finally I couldn't stand it any more. After six months I evaluated the situation and realized that while the Wallach House was spotless and we all wore ironed underwear, we also had one very unhappy little boy. Betty got her pink slip and departed.

Enter nanny number two, Katherine. Networking can be everything sometimes. Katherine was nanny Kathy's roommate. A college graduate and manager of a local jewelry store, she was looking for a change of pace. She has stepped in admirably and for the last two and a half years has been a terrific addition to my support staff. I feel so fortunate to have had the benefit of nanny Kathy and nanny Katherine. They are two young women who have made a real difference in my life.

Because of my experience with Kathy and Katherine, I have become much more interested in the issue of developing affordable, quality day care options in this country. Not everyone has the financial resources that I have been so fortunate to have, and not everyone can have a Kathy or a Katherine, but I'd sure like to ensure that more women at all levels can have at least that kind of quality nurturing care for their children. I'm not sure that our country can afford anything less.

CHAPTER 11. THE (NEW) FACTS OF LIFE

June Cleaver doesn't live here anymore.

"Mommy, don't go. Stay home and play with me," wailed four year-old David-Andrew pitifully, clutching my leg and holding on for dear life.

Dressed for work, briefcase in one hand, car keys in the other and already six minutes late for my 7:30 a.m. meeting, I squatted down next to my little boy so we could talk eye to eye. As I looked into those big hazel eyes, now brimming over with tears, I hugged him tight and, mustering up my cheeriest possible tone of voice, tried to convince him that my leaving was a good idea. "Honey, Mommy has to go to work now. I have to go and bring home the bacon."

"But, Mommy," came his very sad five-year-old reply, "I don't liiiike bacon any more!"

And thus began another day in my balancing act whereby I was executive by day, wife and mother by night, and guilty a good deal of the time - a real Type G personality.

June Cleaver never had to explain to the Beaver why she wouldn't be able to attend his graduation ceremony for Tykes on Trikes, or that she could not get home from Dallas "right now" to see him ride his bike for the first time without training wheels. Harriet Nelson never had to figure out how she could sneak out of her office to attend a 10:00 a.m. Tadpole Waterbaby's demonstration at the YMCA when she had four meetings scheduled that day, an out of town client waiting in the reception area to see her, and the annual budget due at 3:00 p.m. Honestly, where are your role models when you need them?

And what about Donna Reed? I doubt that she was ever prone to those overwhelming attacks of the Working Mother's Guilt Syndrome that plagues today's female breed. She never entertained dark thoughts or brooded about whether her having a job was going to warp her little darlings.

Well, you do have to wonder sometimes - and hope like heck that you're not ruining your kid for life. Most of David-Andrew's little schoolmates are content to play with Legos, plastic dinosaurs, and Teenage Mutant Ninja Turtles. The other night David-Andrew was keeping very busy with some little plastic Fisher Price characters, arranging them around their little tables and chairs.

"What are you doing, honey?" I asked, glancing up over the top of the newspaper.

His answer gives a pretty good clue about his perception about what people do when they get together.

"I'm having a meeting," came the response.

David-Andrew's concept of what constitutes a "normal" family may be slightly more non-traditional than the one many kids have. Here comes another attack of the Guilt Syndrome again! (I know I said I gave up guilt in 1985, but face it, some of this stuff is just genetically based and almost impossible to eradicate entirely!)

With some help from my husband, Alan, I do work pretty hard to keep my priorities straight, and this has proven to be a fairly effective way to help avoid too many attacks of the Guilt Syndrome. When I find that I'm being tugged in all different directions by the events around me and am being pummelled by other folks' demands, regrouping and reexamining my priorities usually helps me sort out the mess. This was especially true the afternoon nanny Kathy called to tell me that David-Andrew was white as a ghost and had been vomiting for hours. My desk was piled high with legal documents and sales literature, deadlines were looming, and we were scheduled to roll out a nation wide sales launch of three new mutual funds in just three weeks.

I grabbed my purse and car keys, never looked back, and met Kathy and David-Andrew at the pediatrician's office. As we waited to see the doctor, I glanced around the waiting room and noticed that while there were several gals in business attire waiting with their offspring, there was not one man in a pin striped Brook's Brother suit. Where are the working fathers? Don't their kids ever get sick? I'm not saying working dads never show up in the pediatrician's waiting room, but I am saying that I've never seen them.

The diagnosis in this case was a troubled hernia that needed immediate attention. One of the top pediatric urologists, familiar with David-Andrew's case, was in Denver, not Wisconsin where we now lived. So with the pediatrician's caution that to postpone surgery could have serious complications and with rushed emergency arrangements made with Denver's Children's

Hospital, we were all on a flight to Colorado two hours after leaving the doctor's office. I could have pleaded that I was too busy to go, that David-Andrew was too little to know if I was there or not and certainly would not remember one way or the other, and Alan (self-employed attorney with a flexible schedule) could have capably taken David-Andrew by himself while I stayed with my shoulder to the grindstone. Are you kidding?

It never crossed my mind that there was anything else to do except for both of David-Andrew's parents to be with him. The country could wait for three more mutual funds. This couldn't. So what could the company do to me? I could just see the headline on the front of *Business Week*, "Mutual Fund Maven and Mom Fired. Skips Work To Attend Son's Surgery." Get real. As it turned out the surgery was successful; our new fund portfolios were launched on time, and the Guilt Syndrome did not strike.

And if it's not the Working Mother's Guilt Syndrome threatening to attack, it's the What I Wouldn't Give For A Trap Door Now Syndrome. The Trap Door Syndrome occurs whenever an executive mom finds herself in a mortifying situation during which she fervently prays that a large, fast-acting spring-operated trap door will open up immediately beneath her; she will disappear from the scene at once and be permanently saved from what could prove to be a fatal Maalox moment.

I have wished for enough trap doors over the past few years to qualify me for some kind of hall of fame, I'm sure. In fact, I experienced the What I Wouldn't Give For A Trap Door Now Syndrome just recently while attending a national financial planning convention. As I was headed to attend the afternoon's key note session, I met Dick Franklin in the hall.

"Dick, hang on a minute. I've got that pension plan proposal format to show you if you have a minute."

Plopping down my briefcase on the nearest table, I undid the clasps, starting to open the case to extract the material for Dick.

Now Dick is an industry superstar of sorts who views himself as a highly sophisticated, terrifically successful national sales manager for another mutual fund. I've known him for years. He's a large guy with lots of dark hair, a big mustache, eyes that bore right through you, enough gold chains to anchor Donald Trump's yacht and the single minded arrogance of a Kamikaze. This guy is Mr. Intimidation personified. Every time I'm around Dick, I feel as though I am about to get hit by a steam roller.

Dick and I had sparred recently at an industry discussion group about a pension proposal format that I had just implemented for our company. In public, in front of several of our mutual peers from other companies, he'd expressed his disdain for what I thought was a pretty innovative new approach to pension marketing, and I was anxious to have him eat his words.

Realizing that we would both be attending this conference, I'd brought a copy of the pension marketing proposal with me and kept my eyes out for him at this convention with the express purpose of showing off our materials and proving him wrong. I knew that if he could get his ego in tow for five minutes, he'd be impressed and maybe even a little envious of our approach, and this was a guy that I have been trying to impress for more than seventeen years. This guy knew me from way back when I started out in the secretarial pool, and now that I was a senior executive, running a company of my own, I desperately wanted to validate myself with him. At last, I was about to get my chance.

Dick stood next to me as I lifted the lid of my briefcase, reached in to extract the beautifully bound proposal that was going to blow him away and ensure a place for me in history as "that smart broad." As our eyes glanced simultaneously into my briefcase what did I see lying right on top of my other work papers in full view of Mr. Intimidation? *The Sesame Street A-B-C Coloring Book* which I had purchased during the break to take home to David-Andrew! Not exactly required reading for financial professionals. Somebody pull the handle on the trap door, please.

One of my very first wishes for a trap door occurred when David-Andrew was still an infant. I was standing in LaGuardia getting ready to make a phone call to the office before I boarded my United flight for home. It was a rainy fall day, so I was wearing my trench coat and was digging through the flotsam in my pockets for a quarter to use in the phone. Just then I heard someone call my name, "Rochelle, hold on, I want to introduce you to someone."

Looking over my shoulder I saw Dan Ashelman, a very successful wholesaler that I had known for years, headed my way with the president of one of the largest money management complexes in the country at his side.

"Rochelle is chief executive of one of the fastest growing mutual funds in the country," Dan began.

I was glowing. Dan was paying me such a nice compliment right here in front of one of the giants of the mutual fund industry.

"It's an honor to meet you, sir," I was saying, with a healthy degree of respect - and no small feeling of admiration - for his accomplishments, as I withdrew my hand from my pocket to offer it in a hand shake.

At the same time I was mortified to realize that the ring of one of David-Andrew's pacifiers, that had been in my coat pocket, was looped around the thumb of my right hand which I was extending toward him. Had this been happening to one of my male colleagues, I told myself, he would have rolls of $20 bills or a twenty-four karat gold money clip engraved with the company logo in his pocket and here the best I could come up with was a lint covered yellow pacifier. I could have used the trap door right then and there.

I know I'm not alone in experiencing the Trap Door Syndrome. A lady I know, Barb, is a trial lawyer. She was just finishing a long controversial jury trial recently and had asked her nanny to bring her little three year old boy, Jeffrey, down to the courthouse so she could treat him to lunch. Jeffrey and the nanny had arrived a little early and had seated themselves in the back of the courtroom to wait for Barb to finish. As Barb concluded her summation, the judge banged the gavel and excused the jury who began to file out.

As everyone rose and began to leave the courtroom, Jeffrey ran to the front of the room to greet his mom. Excitedly waving his little arms he bellowed at the top of his lungs, "Mom, Mom, that guy with the hammer didn't even say 'Oh, shit' like Daddy does when he bangs!" As accurate as Jeffrey's observation was, Barb would have much preferred for this bit of dialogue to have taken place anywhere else rather than in her professional arena in front of all her colleagues and a jury of relative strangers who went to their deliberations snickering and muffling chuckles all the way.

From my observations, working mothers, much more than working fathers, seem to invest a lot of time and effort to create and maintain an entirely professional decorum around their offices. They seem to want to present the facade of corporate dedication personified, the image of someone who is not distracted from the organization's bottom line by anything so mundane as hearth and home. I have caught myself walking that delicate tightrope between wanting to be an available and supportive mom while at the same time not being confident that I had the liberty to portray myself as anything but the consummate professional at work.

Because being a working mother, by definition, meant that I would probably miss some of the important "firsts" in David-Andrew's life - like his first word and first step, nanny Kathy had explicit instructions to call me immediately without fail whenever one of these firsts occurred, so that I could at least vicariously enjoy the moment. As David-Andrew got older, Kathy and I agreed that it would be all right for him to call me at the office on my private line and share the news.

One day as I was having a critical meeting with some of our key senior people - corporate counsel, chairman of the board, head of the audit committee - all rather staid, humorless "grey hairs" - to finalize an important capital expenditure request, my personal phone line rang. Normally, my secretary would have intercepted the call since I was in a "do not disturb" meeting. However, Wendy had stepped away for a few moments to run copies of some of the financial schedules we needed to review in the meeting.

I politely begged everyone's indulgence and excused myself to answer my phone. Planning to quickly brush off the caller with a promise to call them back, I was startled to hear three-year-old David-Andrew's voice on the other end of the line.

"Mommy, Mommy, I've got some great news to tell you. Nanny Kathy said I could call."

"Is that so?"

"Yes. I pooped in the toilet today."

This really was great news, the mom side of me said. I wanted to gush, "Oh honey, that's just wonderful. I'm so proud of you acting like such a big boy," and heap on the accolades, but this was going to take some verbal gymnastics to finish the conversation without revealing its true nature to the gentlemen assembled in my office.

"Well, that certainly is outstanding. Tell me about it."

In his excited little voice, never stopping to take a breath he blurted out, "I told nanny Kathy I had to go number two and she held me on the seat and I went. She says I'm a big boy now. Am I?"

"Yes, indeed and I'm so pleased that you called to inform me. Let me congratulate you on such a fine performance. I knew I could count on you to accomplish this on your own and it deserves the appropriate recognition. We'll definitely need to celebrate this achievement soon. I'm tied up in a meeting right now, but I'll call you back in half an hour so we can discuss it. OK? I'll talk to you later."

"Mommy, Mommy, how long is half an hour? Longer than 'Sesame Street'?"

"Good bye."

"Bye, Mom."

As I hung up the phone, I wasn't sure whether this was a Maalox moment, a Trap Door incident, or an attack of the Guilt Syndrome. I did know that Henry Ford never had to deal with it.

Toilet training is such an important part of every toddler's life and as such, just because you can "escape" to the office all day bodily functions don't turn off at sundown, so the executive mom gets involved in the act. In my case, I'm not sure that this project was one that I helped or hindered. Nanny Kathy, with her nursing background and previous nanny experience, devised what she assured me was a potty training cram course 100 percent guaranteed method to train David-Andrew in five days. She would handle the system during the day, but I was responsible for its success in the evenings. Just the challenge I needed after a hard day at the office, right? As she explained the method to me, logic told me it was an entirely sensible but rather complicated system to train David-Andrew in the civilized ways of disposing of body waste. As it turned out, it was only complicated for me.

The approach she devised involved Dixie cups, Planter's peanuts, water, and M&Ms. Kathy would line up three little Dixie cups on the kitchen counter: lightly salted peanuts in the first cup, water in the second, and the candies in the third. (Are you with me, so far?) The idea was for David-Andrew to eat a few peanuts to get the process going. Because the salty peanuts would make him thirsty, he would soon be ready for the cup or two of water. Shortly after drinking the water, Kathy assured me he would need to use the potty, and when he did he was to be praised lavishly and presented with a little handful of M&Ms as a reward. This system would be operational all day waiting for me to take over when I came home from the office.

Each evening Kathy had the cups all lined up on the kitchen counter for me, and I had been coached in the correct order to administer them. However, David-Andrew's toilet training was being accomplished at the same time that I was organizing a new company and rolling out a new pension and profit-sharing plan campaign. My head was swimming with all the details involved with getting the business going, including the planning of over 100 coast-to-coast kick-off training events.

I would come in the back door, and as I dumped my briefcase and stacks of industry newspapers, mutual fund documents and the other "homework" I'd carried home from the office plus the day's mail on the kitchen counter, everything would spread out in avalanche fashion invariably scrunching the Dixie cups together. Once bunched together, no longer in Kathy's meticulous order, I wasn't at all certain about what cup to use first. I knew every half hour I was supposed to give David-Andrew the contents of a cup, but I couldn't seem to keep it straight as to which cup in what order.

Sometimes he got peanut cups twice in a row, followed by a cup or two of M&Ms, and then two water cups. When by coincidence (it could not have been by design due to my mixing of the cups), he would use his potty I would generally have run out of candy.

"But nanny Kathy always gives me M&Ms," he would wail and I would feel like a total flop.

I often wondered how Peter Lynch would have handled this.

I'm sure Norman Rockwell never had our household in mind when he illustrated the all American family. Our morning family routine sometimes seems like the old Abbott and Costello comedy sketch, "Who's On First", as Alan and I - on our way out - and the nanny - on her way in - converse as we pass each other in the garage at 7:30 a.m.

Alan: "Off to Wausau, back at seven."

Rochelle: "Wait, I'm off to Orlando at three. Won't be back until tomorrow night."

Nanny Katherine: "David-Andrew's got Tadpole swimming at 4:30 p.m. and Termite Hockey at six. I can handle the swim thing, feed him afterwards, then drop him at Karen Hankes' house. She can take David-Andrew and her Matthew to hockey."

Alan: "Great. I'll pick Matthew and David-Andrew up at hockey and bring them home. See you (looking at Katherine) tomorrow morning then. See you (looking at me) tomorrow night sometime."

Rochelle: "Back tomorrow on the 4:15 plane. I'll stop in the office to get my mail and then pick up David-Andrew at Tadpoles. But I've got a 6:30 dinner meeting. Alan, you'll have to do hockey duty. Katherine, just fix lasagna for dinner tomorrow night. Friday night we're having company, but don't worry. Just a few of the directors. One of them's a vegetarian. I'll call you from Florida and we'll plan the menu."

Nanny Katherine: "Thought the party for your top salespeople was Friday."

Rochelle: "Next Friday. Lots to do for that. Need to line up a pianist or harpist. We'll talk about it when I call."

Nanny Katherine: "Alice is coming to clean tomorrow so the house will be fine. Do you still want to have the gutters cleaned? And what about the freezer in the garage? It's not working right."

Rochelle: "Alice, good."

Alan: "Gutters, yes. Freezer, maybe. Call and get a few estimates....talk to you tomorrow morning about it. OK? Got to go or I'll be late. Bye. Love you. Have a good trip . . . oh, by the way, I'm in Milwaukee next Monday and Tuesday."

Rochelle: "OK. Bye. love you, too (to Alan). Have a good day (looking at Katherine). Call you later. Tell Alice to see if she can get that stain off the front stairs carpet and don't use Pledge on the dining room table and we're getting ugly yellow wax buildup on the kitchen floor. So long . . . what did Alan say? Tell him when you see him tomorrow that I'm going to be in Phoenix next week. Never mind, I'll tell him myself when I call tonight. By the way, can you stay overnight Monday night? Have a good one. Bye."

Nanny Katherine: "OK. Sure. I'll check my calendar."

Rochelle: (Sticking head out of window while backing out of driveway.) "Call Elizabeth and see if she can baby-sit Saturday night."

Nanny Katherine: (Now in doorway into house, turning around.) "Sure, what time?"

Rochelle: (Driving off.) "Not sure. Probably 6:00. No, make it 5:30." (Waving.)

Nanny Katherine: (Limp wave.) "Whew."

This logistics nightmare, to a greater or lesser extent, takes place every morning. And not just in our garage. Day-Timers Corporation just hasn't created an adequate product for this two-career-couple-with-family scheduling problem at all. If Apple computer could scale down the programs that map troop movements in the war room at the Pentagon to a family application, I predict there would be a Macintosh in every kitchen in America today!

The demands of home and office are constantly challenging female executives. I'm convinced that we do deal with a different set of obstacles than are presented to men in business. On David-Andrew's third birthday, I found myself in Florida slotted to speak at 10:00 a.m. at a large national financial conference. Together with nanny Kathy, we had planned a dinner hour birthday party for that evening to celebrate the occasion with thirteen of David-Andrew's pals; I had assured him that I would be back in Appleton in plenty of time for all the festivities that were to start at 6:00 p.m.

I made this promise with ardent hopes that the weather in the Midwest would cooperate (Spring in this part of the country can be iffy at best) and that indeed I would make it back on time. After finishing my presentation at 11:15 a.m., I literally bolted from the podium, grabbed my briefcase and luggage which I had stashed in the back of the room, climbed into the hotel limo and hot footed it to the airport in Tampa to catch the 12:37 p.m. plane home. Changing planes in

Chicago, I would arrive back in Appleton at four o'clock, leaving me plenty of time to stop at the office and then head for home and the party.

I arrived at the Tampa airport with plenty of time to spare and sauntered to the gate, boarding pass in hand. As luck would have it, I was informed upon reaching the gate that the flight had been delayed due to bad weather in Chicago, not an uncommon occurrence especially at this time of year. And the projected new departure time would not allow me to make my connecting flight at O'Hare. If I stuck with my original plan, I would not arrive home until well after the cake and ice cream had been served. This would never do.

Pulling out my airline travel guide, I realized that if I could get onto the plane to Atlanta, which left in twenty minutes, fly to St. Louis, catch the flight into Milwaukee and then get the commuter flight home, I could avoid the bad weather in Chicago and get home just in time to greet the children at the door as they arrived. To pull this one off was going to take the choreography of a Broadway musical production and the precise timing of the *Mission: Impossible* crew, but I crossed my fingers and hoped like heck that it would work out just fine. And the first three legs of the trip did.

When I reached Milwaukee, however, the bad weather that had plagued Chicago had crept northward, and my commuter flight had been cancelled. Grabbing my luggage and briefcase, I did an O.J. Simpson dash through the terminal to the Hertz counter where I rented a car, drove twenty miles an hour over the speed limit and pulled into my driveway at 5:50 p.m. Running into the house, I threw my luggage in the corner, ran a comb through my hair, slid some lipstick across my face and opened the front door smiling, hopefully looking relaxed rather than shell-shocked, just as the first mother arrived with her child.

When it came to schedule-juggling and family devotion I had a terrific role model. My mom was a great proponent of supporting her offsprings' interests and activities. I remember in particular one occasion in sixth grade when I was a participant in a spoken poetry contest. Mom and Dad had over 100 guests in camp at the time, so my mother was not able to get into town with me ahead of time and stay for the entire poetry festival. The weather was rotten the day of my big event, so I knew that even Dad's bush pilots wouldn't be flying. I was sure that there was no way that Mom could ever make it on time to hear me recite my three stanzas.

Undeterred by such seeming obstacles, my mother had one of our Indian guides take her five miles over a very choppy lake in an aluminum fishing boat with a fifteen horsepower Evinrude outboard motor, waves crashing over the bow, to the landing at the nearest Indian reservation, where she then bumped over forty miles on a dirt and gravel road with potholes the size of craters in a rusted out pick up truck to arrive at my poetry festival. When I looked out at the audience after I was introduced and had taken the stage, there she sat in the second row looking as fresh as if she had just walked out of Neiman Marcus.

If one of my biggest adjustments early on with integrating a baby into the rest of my life was my before work morning routine, as David-Andrew got older the logistics at the end of the day became every bit as complex. When our son was just an infant and toddler I would come home after work, hug and kiss him, flop in a chair with my feet propped up on a stack of *Wall Street Journal*s, watch some of his cute antics like spraying strained peas through his nose, and put him to bed. Not anymore. Eager for David-Andrew to develop as many skills and interests as he seems keen on, and looking for my only child to have the opportunity to be with other children (some of whom do not have antiques for parents) we have signed him up for Tadpole swimming, Termite Hockey, gymnastics, private Spanish and piano lessons, and - at his demand - judo instruction. This is great, except it does complicate the after work routine just a tad. No more relaxing glass of wine before dinner. Now Alan and I juggle our schedules and agendas with a skill that makes the Karimazov Brothers look like amateurs, in order to make sure someone is available to chauffeur our little tyke around town.

OK, OK, I'll admit that sometimes it does get complicated and we experience brain fade. There has been a time or two when Alan drove clear across town to deliver David-Andrew to his piano lesson only to find out it was the next night, and once we showed up for the Tadpoles swim show a week early. But generally we don't drop many of the scheduling balls. I will admit to you, though, that one of my recurring nightmares is that I am in an empty class room with an oak floor juggling three dozen balls. It's hard work but I catch all the balls, put them in my pocket and walk out the door. Halfway down the hall, I hear the sound of balls hitting the floor in the room I just left. I can think of all sorts of plausible psychiatric interpretations that a shrink could come up with analyzing that dream!

As I'm driving a car load of seven-year-old boys to Termite Hockey, I keep telling myself that this will all be worth it when David-Andrew is accepted to Harvard with a full scholarship for Spanish speaking judo experts who can play Mozart's piano sonatas while shooting hockey pucks across an Olympic sized swimming pool.

Even on nights when David-Andrew's schedule is void of developmental activities, evenings are a riot. Most evenings when I walk in the back door usually dead tired from a tough twelve hour day, I am struck with the eternal truth that working moms don't just have one job, they have three jobs - career, mom, and wife. My idea of heaven would be to come home from the office, sit in the living room while someone poured me a glass of wine, put my feet up as soft fluffy slippers were exchanged for tight leather pumps, and do NOTHING for fifteen minutes. Instead I scurry around serving dinner while David-Andrew tugs at me telling me about what happened at Montessori school that day.

As we sit down to eat, David-Andrew typically continues his monologue, and I gaze at him attentively so he won't feel rejected. As we finish dinner, David-Andrew has about run out of details to impart, slips off his chair and runs into the living room to watch half an hour of the Nickelodeon channel before bedtime. More often than not, at this point Alan, who has been trying to tell me about his day during dinner, sounding exactly like a miffed eight year-old, starts complaining, "I never get any attention. You never listen to me. You don't care."

"Alan," comes the retort, "get a life."

Well, I'm sorry, but after twelve hours at the office, coaching and cajoling salespeople, wrestling with budgets, and watching the market plummet forty-two points in a day, the last thing I am able to do is come home and nurture one more adult. He clearly deserves it and believe me I plan to make it all up to him - and soon.

Alan, like most other male partners of the two career couple with kids, thought he had a life. And he does. It just gets short changed sometimes. National polls show that in situations like ours, the wife's priorities are (1) children, (2) job, and at the very bottom of the list, (3) hubby. So the poor guy sort of gets whatever's left over. During our first three or four years A.C. (after child), I'll admit that what was left over was precious little.

While hustling jobs, David-Andrew, and our travel schedules, Alan and I felt as if we were living our lives as two ships passing in the night. And after David-Andrew's bedtime was about the only time we had for any meaningful interaction of our own. It seemed at times that we were more roommates than soul mates. Unfortunately by the time the dinner dishes were put away, David-Andrew was finally settled for the night and I had completed whatever work I had lugged home from the office, I'd flop into bed exhausted. Totally fatigued from the day's efforts, my libido was completely shut down, and the farthest thing from my mind was romance. For this new mom, the word that described the ultimate sensual experience began with an "S" all right . . . SLEEP.

CHAPTER 12. STRESSED FOR SUCCESS

Where image ends and a crisis begins.

Image counts for a lot in business. Or so image consultants would have us believe. I would argue that performance is everything in business - but image sure doesn't hurt.

Maintaining a professional image is important for both professional men and women in business. It's just that we working moms have some obstacles to overcome that our male counterparts usually never have to deal with.

A professional appearance - well tailored, clean clothes; polished shoes; attractively styled and clean hair; fresh make up - all project the image that you are a competent business person. After awhile I finally got the hang of fixing my hair and makeup in the morning while getting the baby ready, so that I at least looked "together" whether I felt that way or not. Many's the morning, however, when I would be all ready to leave for work when I could not resist the urge to pick up the baby one more time to give him a hug and a kiss before handing him back to nanny Kathy only to find that he had drooled on my shoulder or that he had spit up all down my back.

Back to the closet. I kept the local cleaning economy rolling for years. I'd have "baby cheese" on my sleeves, chocolate handprints on the front of my skirts, and strained beets or carrots crusted on my bosom. And you thought moths were hard on clothes. Hah! You can spray for moths or leave cedar chips in your drawers. Short of living in a cloud of Scotchgard or a plastic bag, there is no way to avoid The Heartbreak of Oatmeal On Your Blazer.

The absolute worst case of Oatmeal On My Blazer, or Academy Award for best clothes destruction by a baby, that I experienced occurred when David-Andrew was about fourteen-months-old. Alan and I had actually gotten away to San Diego for our first few days of vacation since the baby was born. We brought nanny Kathy and David-Andrew along, and they stayed in the room adjoining ours. We enjoyed three wonderful relaxing days basking in the sun, lounging around the pool, and generally fooling around and unwinding. I began to think that I really could handle this executive mom routine after all.

Never one to leave the office totally behind, I had arranged to meet with Jerry Overgaard, one of my regional sales vice-presidents, in San Francisco on our way home. Jerry had insisted on picking us up at the airport and delivering us to the hotel. Since this trip was 90 percent vacation and only 10 percent business, I had brought 90 percent vacation clothes with me and one skirt and blazer to wear when I met with Jerry. The Wallach clan, nanny and all, boarded the 747 to San

Francisco, with Alan, David-Andrew and Kathy casually dressed and me decked out in my business attire - and looking pretty professional if I do say so myself. I had especially chosen this outfit to wear when I visited with Jerry because of all my sales managers he was the most fastidious, conservative, and debonair dresser, and I was certain my skirt and blazer would measure up to his sense of style.

As soon as the plane pulled up at the San Francisco gate, we began the typical traveler's procedure of gathering all our carry on luggage, purses, reading material and shopping bags. Nanny Kathy handed David-Andrew to me while she grabbed the diaper bag from the overhead compartment, and it was during the hand off that he opened his mouth and spewed his morning breakfast of Gerber's oatmeal and strained apples on the left front and shoulder of my blazer. It was so sudden that there was no way to anticipate it. Even if I'd known it was coming, what would I have done? Dropped him in the aisle? Thrown him to the gentleman standing behind me? Now this was not just a gentle little upchuck of a tablespoon of overflow, no this was a violent projectile emptying of three-fourths cup of stomach contents. Major yukky.

There were 200 people standing in the aisles behind us wanting to leave the plane; there was nowhere to go to clean up; I had no other business attire to change into. Trap Door - where are you? Trusting Alan to deal with the luggage and Kathy to deal with the baby, I dabbed at my shoulder with a few tissues that I found in my pocket as I traipsed off the plane and onto the jet way.

Once into the terminal, I headed for the ladies room where I mopped myself up as well as I could with a little washcloth that nanny Kathy had in the diaper bag and doused myself with an Estee Lauder sample I had in my purse to try to mask the odor of baby yuk that was rising from my left shoulder like steam from a compost heap.

My mop up efforts got the biggest chunks, but I still had a big stain spreading over my lapel. I tried to drape a scarf over the area, but as soon as we stepped out onto the curb to meet Jerry, it kept blowing off. So we all presented ourselves, nanny Kathy clutching the baby, Alan loaded down with luggage for four, and me looking like a refugee from *Animal House*, to Jerry, who was dressed immaculately and smelled like he had just had a shower in Aramis. After loading all the luggage in the trunk of his Mercedes 350SE, he insisted that I sit in front with him.

As we whizzed down the freeway into the city, I kept trying to open the window so that the breeze would hopefully dilute the aroma rising from my direction, but Jerry kept closing it as he informed me that the air conditioner was on. I often wondered what he thought about our meeting that day. He never did say anything, but I'm sure he's convinced that either I did not bathe that morning, had mistaken A&D ointment for body lotion, or had never sent my jacket to the cleaners. It is so hard to maintain that professional image with oatmeal on your blazer.

Personal grooming is not the only image problem we working moms wrestle with. Take the issue of the family car. Most men drive a clean, neat sedan to the office. Most working women are stuck with the Mommy Mobile. Ask me how I know.

When David-Andrew was about one and a half, I got a call from two east coast pension consultants whom I had been trying to interest in our asset management capabilities for years to no avail. Out of the blue they called me and expressed an interest in meeting. I was delighted, of course, and we arranged to meet downtown the next morning for breakfast.

Following our breakfast , the two consultants agreed to visit our New York offices to learn more about our investment style and results. This was a good sign that they would refer customers to us if we made the grade, so I was feeling very good about our meeting. I noticed that they had stowed their hanging garment bags behind our booth.

"Are you two flying out this morning?" I queried.

"Yes. As a matter of fact we need to leave for the airport right now so we can catch our 10:30 a.m. flight back to New York."

"Do you have a rental car?"

"No. We just planned to catch the hotel limo."

Now what, I thought to myself. I hadn't planned on taking them to the airport but decided that I needed to at least offer to do so in order not to appear ungracious. To my horror, they accepted at once, and we walked to the hotel entrance where the valet produced my car.

So far, no problem with image. I walked around to the back of the car, so that the consultants could pack their bags in the trunk. As I hoisted the lid and they began to place their bags inside, what should we see: a Port-A-Crib and mattress that I had borrowed and needed to return to a friend, two giant sized boxes of Pampers, a Little Tykes easel, three used disposable diapers - in a plastic bag, but still - , a Richard Scarry book, and a Mattel See & Say. Jamming their bags around the edges they looked at one another as if to say, "Why didn't we take the limo?"

My image continued to deteriorate as we hopped in the car. Consultant number one climbed in the back seat where he was faced with the obligatory car seat. In addition, his traveling companions included a Baggie full of now crushed Cheerios, a grasshopper toy with one wing missing, two Weebles, a Babar book, Mickey Mouse ears, a Dakin stuffed buffalo toy, and a slightly soiled bib.

Consultant number two did not fare much better in the front. He had to maneuver his 190 pound frame around a Walgreen's bag full of Vitte Drops and cough medicine, Oreo cookie crumbs, a Tonka truck, a clean diaper, and a cloth paged book that squawked like a whoopie cushion when he sat on it.

I was somewhat chagrinned by the fact that I was clearly driving a Mommy Mobile and not a sleek, immaculate executive auto, but they never acted as though this was at all unusual. However, I will tell you that during subsequent visits I always cleaned out my car before meeting with them, and they always took the hotel limo!!

I was relating this story to one of the service managers who works for our company and telling her that this is not the sort of thing that someone like John Templeton, founder of The Templeton Funds, would ever encounter or even think to worry about.

"Maybe not," Lynn replied, "but men are not immune to it. Let me tell you what happened to me. I flew into Chicago last August to meet with our fund administrator, a trust officer of one of the biggest banks in the city. The trust officer, Jack, and I met during the morning. Then he offered to take me to lunch and drop me off at the airport afterwards. We walked to the parking lot, Jack in his grey business suit, me in a new pale pink linen skirt and blazer.

"We approached a battered station wagon that I realized was Jack's when he unlocked the car door for me. I started to get in. However, I looked on the seat and it was covered with toys, games, coloring books and an empty Nutter Butter cookie bag. Jack, a family man with six children, quickly scooped up the residue and threw it into the back seat where it joined the other debris left behind by the juvenile members of the household. I sat down, gingerly, and off we went.

"The car was stifling, having sat in the hot sun all morning, and Jack turned on the air conditioner to cool things off. I thought I felt a lump under me but decided that it was probably just a spring in the seat and really didn't pay much attention since Jack and I were talking about the new fund accounting system as we drove. When we reached the restaurant, Jack let me off at the front door while he went to park the car. I got out and was horrified to realize that the lump I had been sitting on in the car was a bright purple crayon which had melted on the car seat and was now permanently affixed to my ensemble. I could have screamed.

"Jack, oblivious male that he is, never even apologized nor offered to have my suit cleaned. What a jerk."

"That's awful," I commiserated.

"It sure is. That crayon never did come out of my suit."

CHAPTER 13. GIVING UP GUILT (REALLY)

The fast track vs. the mommy track.

One of the challenges of being an executive mom is the fact that you are a pioneer. You are blazing the trail. There are not generations of those who have gone before you who have already established some ground rules, some structure, some benchmarks against which you can evaluate your own performance. Nope. It's a lot like space exploration, the new frontier.

You're out there alone, doing the best you can without a clue as to whether your decisions are even close to being right or not. And when you're dealing with kids, the truth is you probably aren't even going to know for another twenty-five or thirty years anyway. You get no reliable immediate feedback, no positive or negative reinforcement for your actions. Every time I make a decision, I feel overwhelmed by the Working Mother's Guilt Syndrome and keep expecting the Guilt Patrol or something to burst through the door like Elliott Ness and cart me off to jail for contributing to the ruin of a minor.

Quite frequently these days, after I've delivered a keynote address to a women's professional organization, I find myself surrounded by women carrying around their own versions of the Guilt Syndrome who want me to tell it like it really is.

"Can you really have it all?" I'm asked.

Well, I guess partly the answer rests on your definition of having it all. For me I feel pretty satisfied with how I'm juggling my dual roles; however, I sense that for many more women the jury on this issue is still out.

For example, take one of the five senior officers of our company who handed me her resignation eighteen months after the founding of our mutual fund organization. She was a vice president who had ten years with the company and managed one of the most demanding operations of our firm. She had done a superlative job in helping build a several hundred million dollar mutual fund management company with several thousand investors.

Maureen would have earned just shy of $60,000 that year (in a small Midwestern town of 60,000 people where $60,000 still spends like $60,000 used to) and the prospects for her to flourish as a top flight mutual fund executive (with the compensation and prestige to match) were exceptional. Maureen told me that she loved her job and I know she did because she took on each new challenge with vigor and enthusiasm, but she just couldn't juggle the demands of supervising one of the most demanding operations in our mutual fund organization, thousands of shareholders, over 2,000 sales representatives, and the equally demanding concerns of her two small boys, ages two and five.

During our conversation Maureen told me that it was too much of a struggle and not worth the stress to try to "do it all." She thought maybe she'd come back to work in a couple of years. We talked about some sort of part-time consulting assignment. For a Chartered Financial Analyst (the recognized designation for portfolio analysts) and a MBA with a concentration in finance, I wondered if this bright, creative woman was not going to go bonkers working out car pool schedules and taking her two year old to the zoo for an enriching experience. She thought she might but was not willing to miss out on the important developing years of her children. It was with a great deal of reluctance that I had to announce her resignation to the rest of the staff.

Maureen is not the only conflicted executive mom I know. My friend Jane walked away from her high flying, $200,000 Wall Street career four years ago. At the "top of her career game" with a jet-setting schedule that had her working in New York Monday through Friday while living in her buffet apartment at a snooty Sutton Place address, and spending weekends in Boston at home with her lawyer husband, Ghanaian nanny and two-year-old daughter Caroline, Jane threw in the towel. Snubbing her nose at corporate life, she put her savings on the line and launched her own Boston-based financial planning practice. She tells me she did it so she could drop in at Caroline's gymnastics class from time to time and put ribbons on her pigtails every now and then during the week instead of just on the weekends.

Then my doctor, Karen Adler-Fisher, gave up, too. In April, when I tried to make an appointment for a physical, her office could not get me in to see her until July. (I could have died by then!) I claimed that it was real emergency and the office squeezed me onto the appointment book. Karen told me while she was looking in my ears that her three-year-old was more then she could handle already and now that she was five-months pregnant with number two, she just couldn't manage anymore.

Karen was so tired all the time that she sometimes thought she was having a nervous breakdown (maybe as a more attractive alternative to the rat race). She felt that she was mean and horrible to her husband most of the time. She said she spent most of her time worrying about how to get rid of her last patient at night, pick up her son from the sitter, stop at Pic 'N Save for groceries, make dinner and arrive at the hospital for rounds at 7:30 p.m. and still get back home to give her little guy a bath and read him a story. Talk about conflicted! Here is a woman who wants to give her son the same security as June Cleaver and her patients the same care as Marcus Welby.

Karen decided the only answer was to cut back her medical practice to half days. Half the income. Half the benefits. Less return on her more than twelve years of higher education. She thinks that this will work out better.

Will it? I don't know. But I do know that misery loves company. As I talk with other women who are struggling to have it all, I realize that I am not the only one who may not exactly have the knack just yet.

So what's the answer? Can you have it all? You can if you understand that it comes with a price, and you decide that you're willing to pay for it. There are big trade offs (and the trade offs aren't the same for everyone) to having it all, and some of us aren't willing or able to sacrifice the time, energy, or dollars it takes.

Do I have the answer? I wish! I don't have one simple, single answer for this dilemma. But I do know that our world sorely needs more bright, capable women running its companies, social agencies, institutions of higher education, and governments. It needs more women computer programmers, business executives, doctors, professors and sales people. It needs more bright capable men, too. As a society we need to figure out how to use the talents of all our citizens, so that we all benefit and that as a class none of us suffer - neither men, nor women - nor especially the children.

Why aren't there more women at the top who have it all? For a lot of us, it's because we jump off the fast track onto the mommy track. It's because we are discouraged by our inability to realize a vision of our society where family, career and happiness can appear in the same sentence. Maybe the bottom line is that having it all can be a whole lot easier if you don't insist on having it all at once!

Until David-Andrew was born, my definition of "having it all" had revolved largely around the satisfactions and challenges of my work. There was a definite career orientation to my view. Moving up the corporate ladder and being on the fast track was what it was all about.

I'll admit it. I wanted to be part of the rat race. What I found out is that if you want to be in the race, you must reconcile yourself to the fact that there may be some other rats in the race with you.

I have always accepted one of the basic business facts of life that working one's way up the corporate ladder has its risks. No guts, no glory; no pain, no gain and all that rot.

Even when things look their rosiest, the political winds may begin to blow the other way. Mentors may move on. Management may change. The market may dictate different strategies. Frankly, people can get canned. In fact, once, while running the rat race I got the black flag that meant "Whoa, you're out!"

Ninety days after David-Andrew's arrival, I found myself smack dab in the middle of a corporate debate regarding the company's direction and strategy. Electing to be assertive, I took on the vice-chairman and chairman of the board, challenged their positions and made an impassioned speech about my strategic vision. I quickly got a lesson in what can happen when you have a difference of opinion with the head honcho of a billion dollar New York Stock Exchange firm. I was summoned back to New York and immediately found out that management had decided that I should be relieved of my duties.

WHAT?

I was shocked, I was outraged. I had knocked myself out to build our money management organization and launch the firm's new mutual fund family. In fact, I'd put much of the enjoyment of my pregnancy and new motherhood on hold in deference to the needs of the company, only to discover that this "sacrifice" was scarcely necessary.

When I should have been resting, I had been whipping up business plans. When I could have been looking through new baby magazines and having a pedicure, I was jetting cross-country meeting with lawyers, advertising and public relations experts, and sales managers. I had "squeezed in" having a baby so as not to upset the company's objectives.

WELL!

I had been deluded by my own illusions of grandeur, by a feeling that I was indispensable, by visions of Superwoman. When I had been deluged by acres of flowers in the hospital sent from the home office (the same people who were now offering me a "severance" package), I was totally convinced that without my august presence the whole place would have gone to Hell.

Wrong, wrong, wrong and WRONG - again.

As with most of life's events which seem devastating at the time, being fired did not prove to be the end of the world. The final result was that I was offered the chance to build a new investment firm from the ground up - a job that has proven to be far superior in responsibility, authority, and prestige to my previous Wall Street affiliation. In addition, I am now able to live in a wonderful community that is perfect for raising a family. All of this adds up to greatly increased job and personal satisfaction that make the small pay cut I took when I traded Wall Street for the Main Street of a small Midwestern town a very worthwhile trade off indeed. I still consider myself on the fast track, but there are aspects of the mommy track that are appealing as well.

As it turned out, getting fired was a prime learning experience for me and clearly influenced my view of corporate loyalty and my definition of having it all.

Career is still very important to me, but I have begun to see the wisdom of balance. After all, a career is only a job, and jobs may come and go but family endures . . . oatmeal on my blazer and all.

But you knew that.

EPILOGUE

The executive summary.

While the struggle to have it all, the challenge to balance career and family, has been limited almost exclusively to female business people for the last two decades, there is evidence that some things may be changing - granted about as slowly as the glaciers moved across middle America - but changing none the less.

The male executive who not only acknowledges that he is a family man, but who also participates as a responsible parent and partner in family matters, may one day replace the corporate dinosaurs who populate most corner offices right now. Headway in that direction is tortoise-like. However, as the consciousness of more businessmen is raised, the rate of progress should accelerate.

I had the opportunity to chuckle about this evolution and how things are changing as the consciousness of one of the partners in one of the largest public accounting firms in Milwaukee was raised significantly recently. Here's how our phone conversation went:

"Rochelle, this is John Scheid. I've got a little problem."

By the sound of John's voice, it sounded more like a big problem. He was in a panic. Calling me from his office 125 miles away, John, a Price Waterhouse partner, was due in my offices in a few short hours to oversee our annual Board of Trustees audit committee meeting.

My board of trustees - composed of such distinguished and august gentlemen as the former Chief Financial Officer of Mobil Oil, the past Chairman of the

United States Military Joint Chiefs of Staff, and the senior economist for one of the nation's largest food processors - meets quarterly to conduct fund business and convenes for a special meeting once a year to review the financial status of the funds and discuss regulatory issues of import. John, representing our accounting firm, always attends to make a formal presentation and to field questions from the trustees. This year the plan was to hold the audit committee meeting and then adjourn to my home for dinner and a social time. John and the trustees would stay in town overnight and depart following breakfast the next morning.

"What's the problem, John?"

"Debby's out of town; the nanny's gone home sick and I don't know what to do with Monica," he explained with exasperation.

Debby, John's wife and an attorney and law professor, happened to be out of town for a few days attending an American Bar Association conference. Monica was entrusted to stay with her capable nanny while John drove north for the audit committee meeting, but the nanny had just been seized with a violent case of the flu. She called John at his office to announce that he needed to come home and stay with the baby RIGHT NOW.

"I don't know who to call to baby-sit. I'll just have to pack her up and bring her with me to Appleton. What am I going to do with her during the meeting?"

I had formed a mental image of Monica sitting on John's lap while he explained to the former Chairman of the Joint Chiefs the formula for calculating management fees and how the pass through provisions work. He was all in a stew. His professional image was being put on the line, and he didn't like it one bit. Debby and the nanny had always taken care of the product of his reproductive efforts. Now here he was face to face with a situation that thousands of working women face daily.

"Look, John, don't worry about it. Bring Monica along. You can leave her at my house with Katherine, our nanny, on your way into town. She'll be just fine."

What I didn't say was," What goes around comes around," but I sure was tempted.

"Thanks, Rochelle. I'm leaving right now. See you in a few hours."

John hung up, greatly relieved.

I wondered later if this incident raised John's consciousness or whether it would just become another funny story that he would embellish with each telling around the poker table about how he had to pick up the pieces when the nanny pooped out. My prediction is that due to this brief low level domestic crisis (Really this was not exactly a major Trap Door event. Face it, he didn't even have any oatmeal on his blazer.), he will look at his wife, the nanny, and all the women in his office in a different light because that day he found out, if only briefly, that having it all really means managing it all.

Right.

And leopards can change their spots.

Rochelle Lamm Wallach

ABOUT THE AUTHOR

Rochelle Lamm Wallach

A parent since 1985 (and business and baby juggler since then), Rochelle is president of AAL Capital Management Corporation, a billion dollar mutual fund organization. She directs the company's operations through her firm's Appleton, Wisconsin, home office staff and a national sales organization of over 2,000 Registered Representatives. Before founding AAL Capital Management Corporation for a large insurance company in 1986, Rochelle held executive sales management positions with two well known New York based financial services firms for whom she created and introduced new financial products and directed national sales and marketing efforts.

Rochelle is the author of the investment industry best-seller, *On The Road Again: How To Succeed In The Competitive World Of Wholesaling*. This book is now in its third printing and has been used by many of the leading investment and insurance companies in the country as a basis for wholesaler training and development. She co-authored *The Complete Seminar Selling Manual*.

Rochelle holds a BA from Loretto Heights College, an MBA from the University of Denver and was one of the first few hundred individuals in the U.S. to earn the Certified Financial Planner professional designation. Much sought after as a speaker at financial industry conferences and events, she is a popular presenter to women's groups across the country. Rochelle is also the co-founder of the Fox Cities Children's Museum, demonstrating her commitment to family values and community involvement. She is active in the Young President's Organization and is listed in *Who's Who of American Women*.

Rochelle, her husband, Alan, and son, David-Andrew, currently live in Appleton, Wisconsin, where Rochelle was recently named Woman Manager Of The Year.

ABOUT THE CO-AUTHOR

Linda M. Koe

Co-author Linda M. Koe has been a parent since 1966 and has more than 15 years of experience combining kids and career. Linda is president of her own sales and marketing consulting firm, Kirkwood Marketing. In her previous life as a financial services professional, she was a stock broker and held officer and senior management positions with several large and well known bank and mutual fund organizations.

Linda holds an undergraduate degree from the University of Illinois, attended graduate banking school at the University of Oklahoma and is a Certified Cash Manager. She has never been accused of being pregnant and chic, worries that never practicing Lamaze may have interfered with the proper mother-child bonding process, and is prone to frequent guilt attacks that her brand of motherhood may explain why neither of her children have expressed any interest whatsoever in becoming parents themselves.

A resident of Wisconsin, Linda lives with her husband, Bruce, a printing industry executive, in Racine.

Yes! Oatmeal On My Blazer says it all . . .
I need more copies.

☐ *Oatmeal On My Blazer* is great.
☐ I can really relate.
☐ I know others who can relate.
☐ I gave up trying to have it all.
☐ I still don't have it all, but I'm trying.
☐ I'd like to order additional copies for my
family, friends and business associates.

Please send me _____ copies of *Oatmeal On My Blazer* at $9.95 each (plus tax and postage - see below).

Name _____

Address _____

City_____ State_____ Zip_____

Phone (Daytime) _____ (Evening)_____

My check for $9.95 for each book plus $3.00 for postage and handling
(a total of $12.95 per book) is enclosed. Wisconsin residents, please include 5% sales tax.

Cut out this page and send it with your check, payable to Panache Publications, to:

Oatmeal On My Blazer
Panache Publications, 1737 Reid Drive, Appleton, WI 54914

Tell us how you're trying to have it all.
We'd like to know!

Your funny story or anecdote may become part of our next publication, *Oatmeal On Your Blazer: How America's Working Mothers Are Struggling To Have It All.*

America's working moms want to know how you're coping with oatmeal on your blazer. Tell us about your attempts to keep the "having it all" myth alive:

_____

_____

_____

_____

_____

_____

_____

_____

If you need more room, attach another sheet of paper. Your responses will be kept completely confidential if you prefer. However, we would like to know who you are. Please complete the following:

Name _____

Address _____

City_____ State_____ Zip_____

Phone (Daytime) _____ (Evening)_____

☐ You may use my name in *Oatmeal On Your Blazer.* ☐ I prefer that you not use my name.

Cut out this page and send your precious "Oatmeal Moments" to:

Panache Publications, 1737 Reid Drive, Appleton, WI 54914

- FOLD HERE -

FROM:

_____

_____

_____

Place First Class Stamp Here

TO:
Oatmeal On Your Blazer
Panache Publications
1737 Reid Drive
Appleton, WI 54914